RMS EMPRESS OF BRITAIN

BRITAIN'S FINEST LINER

Clive Harvey

TEMPUS

EMPRESS
OF BRITAIN

42.500 GROSS TON...
5 DAY ATLANTIC
GIANTESS

This book is dedicated to the memory of those men
who lost their lives aboard the *Empress of Britain* on
Saturday 26 October, 1940.

The *Empress of Britain* was a most remarkable liner,
a combination of tradition and modernity: upright and imposing,
yet curiously rakish. It was a profile that could only have been
British, and yet, internally she was, and remains, quite unlike any
other British liner: striking and dramatic, yet remarkably elegant.
She has been described as being the most confidently grand liner,
and this is indeed an apt description. She was, without doubt, a liner
of her times: that opulence and grandeur would have hardly fitted
into the brave new world of the 1950s.

First published 2004

Tempus Publishing Ltd
The Mill, Brimscombe Port
Stroud, Gloucestershire Gl5 2QG

© Clive Harvey, 2004

The right of Clive Harvey to be identified as the Author of this work has been asserted in
ccordance with the Copyrights, Designs and Patents Act 1988.

British Library Cataloguing in Publication Data.
A catalogue record for this book is available from the British Library.

ISBN 0 7524 3169 2

Typesetting and design by Liz Rudderham.
Origination by Tempus Publishing.
Printed in Great Britain.

ACKNOWLEDGEMENTS

My thanks go to Luis Miguel Correia for the loan of several important
items, without which there would be no book! My thanks also to
Campbell and Janette McCutcheon for the loan of many photographs
from their collection.

CONTENTS

CANADIAN PACIFIC: THE EARLY YEARS

When Oberleutnant Berhard Jope, pilot of a long-range-four-engined Focke-Wulf Condor 200, fixed the *Empress of Britain* in his sights, the fate of what was arguably Britain's most magnificent ocean liner was sealed. There was little chance that even with her reasonable turn of speed, or with her armament of Lewis guns, that the Canadian Pacific flagship would be any match for the powerful and sophisticated aircraft loaded with up to six 550lb high-explosive bombs.

The story of the *Empress of Britain* has its beginnings in the late 1800s. The first ships owned by the Canadian Pacific Railway to cross the Atlantic were the *Algoma*, *Alberta* and *Athabaska*. Far from being transatlantic liners, these three steamers, of around 2,800 tons, were ordered from shipbuilders on the river Clyde to transport both men and supplies required for the construction work of the great trans-continental railway across Canada, along the northern part of Lake Superior. The Canadian Pacific Railway Co. had been incorporated on 16 February 1881 to build a railway across Canada and work on the creation of the railway was begun just under three months later, on 2 May 1881. It was necessary to provide a means of transportation for the workers building the section of the line that would run along the north shore of Lake Superior, and the three ships had been ordered specifically for this role. The ships, having made their own way across the North

Atlantic as far as Montreal, being too large to negotiate the locks of the St Lawrence and Welland Canals, were then cut into sections and towed to Buffalo. There, the ships were reassembled, and inaugurated Canadian Pacific's Great Lakes service in 1884. Thus, Canadian Pacific's maritime beginnings were indeed modest, if not remarkable.

The *Algoma* was to last in service only a few short months, being sunk during a storm on 7 November the following year, with the loss of forty-eight lives. By contrast, her sister ships lasted until 1948, albeit by that time under different ownership. The construction of the railway took until 7 November 1885 when the great undertaking was completed. However, it was not until the evening of 28 June 1886 that the first train departed Montreal for Port Moody (Vancouver), a journey that took five-and-a-half days to complete.

The summer of 1886 was indeed a significant time for Canadian Pacific, as in July the 800grt sailing vessel, *W.B. Flint*, arrived in Port Moody with a cargo of tea for shipment via the newly established Canadian Pacific Railway. This set in motion the beginnings of what was to become a vast transportation company of railway, ships and aircraft that would all but span the globe. As the work on the transcontinental railway was nearing completion Canadian Pacific had turned their attention to the Pacific Ocean, and begun to draw up plans for a liner service linking Canada with the Orient. In 1887 they chartered three ships: the 3,650grt *Abyssinia*, the 2,549grt *Batavia* and the 3,656grt *Parthia*, and it is these three liners that hold the distinction of having inaugurated the ocean services of Canadian

The first *Empress of Britain* in 1907.

Pacific. They were, however, merely a tentative step towards the company's plans for a regular liner service across the Pacific. In 1889 the company signed a mail agreement with the Post Office, and a clause in this agreement that specified that the ships employed should have a speed of 17½ knots made it clear that new ships would have to be built. An order was placed with the Naval Construction & Armaments Co. of Barrow-in-Furness and the three ships that were built were the first Empress liners. The first to be completed was the *Empress of India*, in January 1891. Her sister vessels, *Empress of Japan* and *Empress of China*, followed in March and July of that same year respectively. At 5,905grt the three new ships were significantly larger than the chartered tonnage but despite their size the ships presented an elegant and graceful profile, with clipper bows, counter sterns and two centrally placed funnels, and three masts. They each had accommodation for 180 passengers in first class, 32 in second and 600 in steerage. Rather than send the ships to Yokohama empty on their delivery voyages, Canadian Pacific promoted the voyage as part of a round-the-world trip, with calls at Gibraltar, Naples, Port Said, Suez, Colombo, Penang, Singapore, Hong Kong, Woosung, Nagasaki and Kobe. The ports would become very familiar in later years to their magnificent flagship, *Empress of Britain*, as she made her annual cruise around the world.

Unfortunately, the *Empress of China* would not enjoy such a long life as her sisters, ultimately being wrecked at Yokohama in July 1911.

With the new 'Empresses' established on the Pacific, some of the company's 'stop-gap' vessels were disposed of. Then, in 1897, the Klondyke gold rush gave the company the opportunity to extend their area of operations by establishing a coastal service between Vancouver and Victoria. They bought the fleet of the Canadian Pacific Navigation Co. and also acquired the Union Line steamers, *Tartar* and *Athenian*. However, it was by now obvious to the company that it was the right time to extend even further, by operating a transatlantic service, and a major step was made in this direction on 27 March 1903, when they announced that they had purchased the Beaver Line and the fifteen ships of their fleet. A service was established from Liverpool, Avonmouth and London, and was later extended to include Antwerp. Beaver Line's principal rival on the Atlantic was Allan Line and, once Canadian Pacific took control of Beaver Line, this rivalry intensified. In order to both strengthen its position and to retain the mail contract, Allan Line ordered two new liners, *Victorian* and *Virginian*. Canadian Pacific rose to the challenge by placing an order with the Fairfield Shipbuilding & Engineering Co. of Govan, Glasgow, for a pair of liners; ships that would become the pioneer Atlantic 'Empresses'; *Empress of Britain* and *Empress of Ireland*. Twin-screw, twin-funnelled liners, they were both of 14,190grt, and proved to be more than a match for the new Allan Line ships. Allan Line then had plans for even larger ships but these had to be shelved due to the high cost. Instead, they moved two other vessels, the 11,000grt *Corsican* and *Grampian*, onto the Canadian service. However, by this time there were signs of a compromise in the operations of both the Allan and Canadian

Pacific fleets, with the mail contract being shared between *Victorian*, *Virginian* and the new 'Empresses'. This eventually led to the two companies being amalgamated in January 1916.

Expansion into the Atlantic trade, and then the loss of the *Empress of China*, led the company towards ordering a further pair of liners for the Pacific. Once again the order was placed with the Fairfield Shipbuilding & Engineering Co. The ships, the largest and finest yet built for Canadian Pacific, were the *Empress of Russia* and *Empress of Asia*. They entered service in April 1913 and June 1914 respectively. Both vessels were of 16,900grt and were capable of 20 knots. Thus, their size, speed and luxurious accommodation ensured that Britain once again was restored to its pre-eminent position on the Pacific. The heavily subsidised liners of Japan's Toyo Kisen Kaisha had begun to seriously undermine this position.

FROM TOP LEFT

The *Empress of China* on her sea trials off Gourock.

The purchase of the Beaver Line in 1903 saw the real start of Canadian Pacific as a transatlantic company. Here is *Lake Champlain* at Liverpool.

With a misspelt name added to her bow, this is most likely the ill-fated *Empress of Ireland* rather than her similar sister.

On her speed trials on the Firth of Clyde, *Empress of Russia* shows a turn of speed as smoke belches from her funnels.

Canadian Pacific suffered a tragic loss in May 1914, when the *Empress of Ireland* was sunk, with the loss of 1,024 lives, after colliding off Father Point in the St Lawrence with the Norwegian collier, *Storstad*. Then, three months later the world was plunged into the horror of war and, as with most shipping companies, nearly all of the Canadian Pacific fleet were requisitioned for war service. *Empress of Britain* was initially converted into an armed merchant cruiser, being used in this role in the Atlantic until May 1915, when she was turned into a troop transport. The Pacific 'Empresses' were also taken over for naval service. The *Empress of India* was later purchased by the Maharajah of Gwalior and turned into a hospital ship: the cost of her operation and maintenance being borne by Indian princes. (After the war she was sold to the founders of the Scindia Steam Navigation Co. and inaugurated the first Indian-owned steamship service). The *Empress of Japan* only briefly saw war-work. Having been commissioned at Hong Kong in August 1914, she was returned to commercial service in October 1915 – remaining in service until 1922. The auxiliary cruiser squadron operated both *Empress of Russia* and *Empress of Asia* but by 1918 they were being used on the Atlantic as transports for American troops.

At the time war was declared Canadian Pacific had under construction two 12,400grt liners, the *Missanabie* and the *Metagama. Missanabie* was completed in September 1914 but was sadly lost to a torpedo attack in the last months of war in September 1918. *Metagama* was more fortunate, having been completed in March 1915: she remained in service until April 1934.

Canadian Pacific had, in all, carried over one million troops and passengers during the four years of conflict as well as carrying four million tons of cargo and munitions. In the midst of the war, in January 1916, Canadian Pacific and Allan Line had merged, with sixteen ships being transferred to the Canadian Pacific fleet, and several of these became war losses.

In the early years after the war, several of the older surviving Allan Line cargo vessels were sold for scrap, being replaced by second-hand tonnage as well as new ships. Losses of passenger vessels also had to be made up, and again, in order to meet the situation until new ships could be built, four former German liners were bought from the Shipping Controller. The *Kaiserin Auguste Victoria* was renamed *Empress of Scotland*; the *Konig Friedrich August* became *Montreal* and the *Prinz Friedrich Wilhelm* was renamed *Montlaurier*. The splendid 21,498grt *Tirpitz*, which was under construction for Hamburg–America as war was declared, was acquired by Canadian Pacific in July 1921, and was at first renamed *Empress of China*. However, the following year, after lengthy alterations, she was given the name *Empress of Australia*. This liner, upon which the Kaiser is believed to have had plans to undertake a victory cruise around the world, instead served Canadian Pacific well, both as a liner and as a cruise ship, for thirty years.

Canadian Pacific took delivery of eight new liners between 1920 and 1929. The first of the post-war liners to be completed was the 21,517grt *Empress of Canada*, which was built for the trans-Pacific service between Vancouver and Yokohama. *Montcalm*, the first of a trio of liners, followed in

1921 and her sister vessels, *Montrose* and *Montclare*, entered service the following year. (In 1924 these ships were joined by the first *Empress of Britain*, which was renamed *Montroyal*.) In 1928 the *Duchess of Bedford*, *Duchess of Atholl* and the *Duchess of Richmond* all entered the company's service. The *Duchess of York*, the final ship of the quartet, was delivered in 1929. Between 1927 and 1928, five Beaver-class cargo steamers were also delivered to the company's Beaver Line subsidiary. The next passenger ship to join the Canadian Pacific fleet was the 26,032grt *Empress of Japan*, in June 1930. Her handsome, three-funnelled profile and splendidly appointed passenger facilities meant that she eclipsed the *Empress of Canada*, which had been received with great acclaim by the travelling public at the beginning of the decade. As in the years before the war, competition on the Pacific service was intense. At the time *Empress of Japan* was under construction in Glasgow the Nippon Yusen Kaisha liners *Asama Maru* and *Tatsuta Maru* were also being built in Nagasaki, and their slightly larger running mate, *Chichibu Maru*, at Yokohama. As the 1920s had progressed so had advances in marine engineering developed rapidly. While the planned Japanese liners would be motor vessels, they would have a maximum speed of 21 knots, making them faster than the turbine steamer *Empress of Canada*. It was therefore decided that the *Empress of Canada* would be re-engined, and she sailed from Vancouver in November 1928 back to her builders yard for the work to be undertaken. Fitted with

OPPOSITE

Empress of Canada, the first of the post-war CPR ships, on her trials on the Clyde.

Montcalm, with the schooner *Wester*, on the Clyde in 1921.

ABOVE

The tug/tender *Bison* at Liverpool, with the *Montclare*, on 6 July 1923.

RIGHT

Duchess of Atholl flying the Wm Beardmore house flag on 5 June 1928 before her handover to Canadian Pacific in 1928.

new, geared turbines, she was able to steam at a maximum speed of 22½ knots. The Atlantic liners, *Montcalm*, *Montclare* and *Montrose*, were also fitted with new, geared turbines, in 1928, 1929 and 1931 respectively.

Canadian Pacific became involved in the cruise business in the early 1920s. While some of their Atlantic liners were placed under charter to travel agencies, operating often quite lengthy cruises, in 1924 Canadian Pacific themselves sent the *Empress of Canada* on a World Cruise. Such was the success of this cruise that it became an annual event through the remainder of the 1920s. However, after the one cruise by the *Empress of Canada* these cruises were then operated by the Atlantic ships *Empress of Scotland*,

It was envisaged that this liner would lure these passengers to Quebec to board the liner rather than face the longer rail journey to New York to board another liner bound for Europe. Canadian Pacific were already promoting their Atlantic service with the slogan, '39% less ocean by the St Lawrence Route.' Thus, the new liner was conceived as a very serious contender to those Manhattan-based liners and would therefore need to be their equal in every possible way. A liner of such luxury would undoubtedly also become the ship of choice for those people taking a World Cruise. The size of the proposed liner was limited by the harbour facilities at Quebec, and the need for her to pass through both the Suez and Panama Canals.

The last of the Duchess quartet, *Duchess of York*, at Liverpool.

Empress of France and *Empress of Australia*. By their very nature, the cruises, lasting in excess of 130 days and with fares beginning at $2,000, were designed for the very wealthy. While the *Empress of Australia*, which operated four such cruises, was undoubtedly opulently appointed, she was nevertheless a liner of pre-war design.

So, in 1927, when the directors of Canadian Pacific decided to build a new liner in a further attempt to capture some of the tourist traffic from the west and middle-west of the United States and Canada, they also decided to equip the ship to make her suitable to undertake the annual World Cruise.

Having made the decision, things moved quite fast and the order for the liner was placed with the John Brown shipyard on the Clyde. Given the yard number 530, the first keel plates were laid on 28 November 1928.

Several months later a delegation of travel and ticket agents from both Canada and the United States were invited by Canadian Pacific to visit the John Brown's yard to see the initial stages of construction of the liner. They were also asked to make suggestions about the layout and the facilities of the ship, and ultimately several of the proposed ideas were incorporated.

*Empress of Japan c.*1929.

Ready to leave for the trip down the Clyde, *Empress of Japan* looks resplendent in her fresh white paint in John Brown's Clydebank fitting out basin.

The opulent Long Gallery aboard the *Empress of Japan*.

The Birth of an Empress

'More than size and speed — space! Space for the individual passenger! That is the new idea in ocean travel which comes with the Empress of Britain.' *His Royal Highness the Prince of Wales was the first to suggest the importance of this ship. He said at her launching: 'This vessel can be considered in construction as the last word in shipbuilding, and as regards her appointments — she will have no rivals.'*

Canadian Pacific brochure, 1931

June 1930 was an important month for Canadian Pacific; the *Empress of Japan* was delivered on 8 June from the Fairfield yard and, as she made her way down the river to the sea, she passed the sparkling white hull of the *Empress of Britain* on the stocks, being made ready for her launching three days later, on the eleventh.

Construction of the hull number 530, which would ultimately become *Empress of Britain*, had progressed well so that by the time the ship was ready to be launched a considerable amount of joiner-work and internal fitting had already been completed. While it was usual for ships to be launched by women, in this instance there was a break with tradition, and the hugely popular Prince of Wales had agreed to perform the naming ceremony. The

Entering the Gladstone Dry Dock in Liverpool after her successful sea trials.

Prince in fact held the title Master of the Merchant Navy, so it was quite appropriate that he should name the ship. With several major liners under construction in Europe and elsewhere in the world at the time, the launching of such a prestigious liner, and by such a popular and glamorous member of the royal family, ensured an aura that exceeded mere national importance. As a result, as well as being covered by the world's press, the launch proceedings were broadcast throughout the British Empire and several other countries. It was the first time that such an event had been covered in this way, and it set the whole tone of modernity and glamour that would surround the ship during her career. A crowd of over 20,000 had gathered to watch the already magnificent hull take to her natural element. At the front of the launch platform the Prince of Wales was flanked by E. W. Beatty, chairman and president of Canadian Pacific, and Lord Aberconway, chairman of John Brown's. There was a brief delay in the ceremony, then once the 'all clear' was given the Prince named the ship and wished success to her and all that sailed in her. Then, having cut the red, white and blue ribbon, a bottle of Canadian wine swung out and smashed against the hull. He pulled a lever that set in progress the release gearing mechanism. Slowly at first, the newly named *Empress of Britain* began to move down the slipway to the cheers of the crowds. Within moments she was afloat, and then was taken in tow by tugs to the fitting out berth where she would be completed.

As the months passed, work continued on the fitting out of the new Empress and the world was plunged ever deeper into Depression. As the

Proud suppliers advertised the use of their products in the Empress. Colvilles supplied much of the steel from their Lanarkshire furnaces and rolling mills.

BELOW LEFT
Her first captain, R.G. Latta.

BELOW RIGHT
HRH The Prince of Wales arriving at John Brown's to launch the *Empress of Britain*.

Empress of Britain neared completion, elsewhere in the John Brown yard work was progressing on the initial construction stages of another prestigious Atlantic liner, vessel 534, which would ultimately become the *Queen Mary*. Eight months after the *Empress of Britain* steamed majestically away from her builders yard, work would cease on the hull of the new Cunarder. Meanwhile, Canadian Pacific were optimistic that the additional mid-west United States traffic would help them override the gloomy prevailing conditions.

In December 1930 Canadian Pacific announced that Captain R.G. Latta would be the master of the new liner. The appointment was a popular choice, as Captain Latta was respected by his crews and well-liked by the passengers. He had joined Canadian Pacific in 1904, and had taken command of the earlier *Empress of Britain* in 1923.

By late March 1931 the fitting out of the magnificent new *Empress of Britain* was nearing completion. Her departure from the shipyard for her trials voyage was timed for early on the afternoon of Sunday 5 April, and a

crowd of several hundred thousand people lined both banks of the river Clyde to take advantage of the opportunity to see the new liner depart on her first voyage out to sea. Special trains were provided by the railway companies to take some of the people to stations near good vantage points while other people arrived by buses and other vehicles, and of course, on foot. All were anxious to see the liner that had gradually dominated the skyline of the John Brown shipyard. Now, at last, she was completed, and she presented a magnificent sight, combining both tradition and modernity. She had an almost straight stem, which seemed an echo of an earlier age, and yet she boasted a stylishly modern cruiser stern. The forward superstructure, while attractively stepped, was uncompromisingly angular and added to the somewhat heavy look to the ship. She was topped by three very large, buff-coloured funnels, each one of which was 68ft high. Around the funnels were clustered several large ventilators and these, as well as her masts and cargo handling gear, were also painted the same shade of buff as the funnels. The twenty-six teak, canvas-covered lifeboats gleamed with varnish. Along her hull, at C-Deck level was a blue sheer-line and she had green boot topping. She looked, every inch, an Empress: regal, elegant and impressive. She was a beacon of splendour, confirmation that the skill and ingenuity of the shipbuilders, craftsmen and artists had not been stifled by the dark days of the Depression.

It took four tugs of the Clyde Shipping Co., *Flying Spray*, *Flying Foam*, *Flying Kite* and *Flying Eagle*, 2½ hours to tow the liner as far as the Tail of the Bank, the deep-water area where the river meets the Firth of Clyde. The Anchor Line tender, *Paladin*, escorted this procession while low-flying aeroplanes buzzed overhead. The tugs were cast off at Princes Pier and the *Empress of Britain* steamed for Holy Loch for the preliminary compass adjustments. Later, she was anchored off Greenock, making a magnificent sight, brilliantly illuminated throughout the evening. The following day anchor trials and steering gear tests were made and the ship returned to her anchorage. It was on 7 April that the *Empress of Britain* sailed for Liverpool. Once there she was berthed at the Gladstone Graving Dock to have her hull inspected, cleaned and painted. She was, at that time, the largest white-hulled liner in the world. With the cleaning and painting of the ship completed she left the Mersey on Saturday 11 April for her full-power, fuel-consumption and manoeuvring trials. To the disappointment of many

Views inside one of the engine rooms.

LEFT
The *Empress of Britain* was fitted with two pairs of propellers made of solid bronze. One pair was 19ft 3in in diameter and weighed 25 tons each, while the smaller set was 14ft in diameter.

BELOW
Her rudder, one of the largest cast, on its route from Darlington to Clydebank.

observers who had gathered at Skelmorlie, the well-known vantage point along the Firth of Clyde, from where speed trials were often held, the *Empress of Britain* headed further along the coast, carrying out her speed trials off the coast of the Isle of Arran. During the two days of exhaustive tests the sea was rough and there was a strong breeze but, despite these weather conditions, the liner performed well, exceeding her contract speed of 24 knots and reaching an average speed of 25.271 knots. A feature that struck many on board during the trials was that whether under full power or cruising conditions, the smoothness and lack of vibration and noise made it difficult for them to realise that such great power and speed was being developed. The tests continued and in all, over the seven days the *Empress of Britain* sailed

1,700 miles in all manner of sea conditions. The representatives of both John Brown's and of Canadian Pacific that had been aboard to take note and evaluate every nuance of her performance were impressed by the results. They were convinced that in the *Empress of Britain* they had a winner.

On completion of the trials the new Empress was handed over to Canadian Pacific at Greenock. Proudly flying the Canadian Pacific house flag she was turned southwards towards Southampton. Her arrival there on 16 April was greeted by further crowds all anxious to see Britain's newest and most splendid ocean liner. She was due to depart on her maiden voyage on 27 May. The publication *The Shipbuilder and Marine Engine-Builder* reported: 'The speed of the ship is such that she will make the passage from

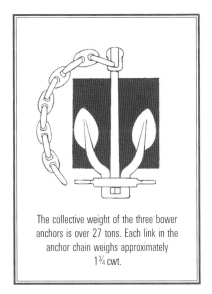

Viewed from the air, the *Empress of Britain* sails off Wemyss Bay on her speed trials.

The collective weight of the three bower anchors is over 27 tons. Each link in the anchor chain weighs approximately 1¾ cwt.

Southampton to Quebec in five days, but the actual open Atlantic stretch will only occupy three-and-a-half days. With her great reserve of power, she will be able to maintain her schedule speed steadily even under extremely adverse weather conditions. It may be anticipated with confidence that the *Empress of Britain*, in addition to forging one more proud link between the Mother Country and the great Dominion of Canada, will mark another notable conquest of the Atlantic – a conquest which would have been impossible but for the marvellous progress made in marine engineering during the past decade.'

The *Empress of Britain* was built to conform to the requirements of Lloyd's Register of shipping, under that society's highest class +100A1. She had ten decks, one of which, the Promenade Deck, was 648ft long. Above the Promenade Deck was the Boat Deck; above this the Sports Deck, and then the topmost deck, the Sun Deck, from which rose the tops of the funnel casings, ventilators and other portions of the superstructure. Below the Promenade Deck, and running the full length of the ship, was the first of the decks contained within the hull, lettered from A to G. The two lowest decks, F and G, did not extend the entire length of the ship, but only forward and aft the machinery space.

The whole of the steel plating below the waterline was doubled, the distances between the inner and outer plates or skins varying from 4ft at the sides to just over 5ft in way of the centre line. Between the inner and outer plating, subdivided into forty-four main compartments, oil fuel was carried, along with reserves of fresh water and water ballast. The main bulk of the oil fuel for the boilers was carried in huge tanks which were arranged at the sides and ends of the boiler rooms.

Although every effort was made to reduce weight with the use of special steels, the hull was of remarkably strong construction. The flat plate keel comprised two layers of steel plating, which together were over 2in thick. Amidships, the outer plating of the bottom and sides was just less than 1in thick, and extensive hydraulic riveting was used. An interesting feature of the hull construction was the doubling of the forward water-line plating for a length of 150ft from the stem, as a protection against floating ice that may be encountered in the St Lawrence. Between A Deck and the Promenade Deck the side plating was doubled. The total weight of the steel in the hull alone was over 19,000 tons. Some of the steel used took the form of huge steel castings, such as those for the stern post, carrying the rudder, the brackets that supported the propeller shafts, and part of the stem. The stern post and shaft castings, together, weighed about 130 tons. Her enormous rudder and stock comprised steel forgings weighing 65 tons, covered on either side with steel plating. The rudder forging was built up in Darlington, Co. Durham, and was transported on a special sixteen-wheel lorry to the shipyard. The journey, which had required careful planning of the route as well as handling of the load, took seven days.

She was designed with a most elegant cruiser-type stern, and yet she had an ordinary straight stem. The stem was a rolled steel bar carried up from a casting at the forefoot. A further point of design was the use amidships of two huge beams, which provided a clear space, 60ft long, 60ft wide and 19ft high, in the middle of the first-class dining saloon. The beams rested on side pillars that served as ventilators to the machinery space.

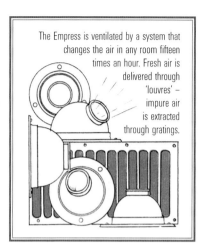

The Empress is ventilated by a system that changes the air in any room fifteen times an hour. Fresh air is delivered through 'louvres' – impure air is extracted through gratings.

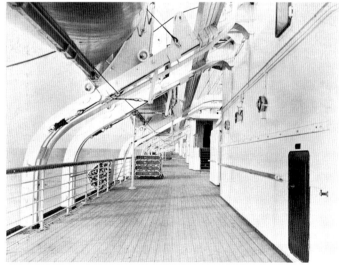

There were eighteen lifeboats, each 30ft 10in long by 10ft wide, with a carrying capacity of eighty-nine passengers and crew.

Empress of Britain was, of course, built to the very highest standards of safety, being subdivided by fourteen transverse bulkheads extending up to D Deck. The inner sides of the engine room and boiler room tanks provided additional subdivision, with the aft portion of G Deck constituting a watertight covering over the respective propeller shaft tunnels. The bulkheads were pierced by large openings that could be closed by watertight doors. In the event of an emergency all the watertight doors could be closed simultaneously from the bridge. An alarm signal at each door gave a warning when it was about to be closed, and an electric light indicator in the chart-room showed whether the doors were closed or open. Above D Deck, where the watertight bulkheads terminated, the whole ship was subdivided by fireproof bulkheads and provided with fire-resisting doors. In addition to her fireproof bulkheads the ship was provided with an elaborate system of protection against fire. In all corridors, and at vital points, were placed chemical extinguishers for hand use. There were also numerous hydrants for the supply of water from special pumps to fire hoses. Ample warning of fire or any other emergency was given to passengers and crew by a system of fifty-eight electric horns placed in suitable positions throughout the ship. In addition, the cargo holds were protected from fire by means of a special smoke-detecting instrument in the wheelhouse, which gave immediate indication of the slightest traces of smoke in any of the cargo spaces. In the event of a fire breaking out in the cargo, the hold, or holds, could be flooded with carbon-dioxide gas. A similar system was provided to deal with fire in any of the machinery rooms.

An extensive range of life-saving equipment was carried: there were eighteen lifeboats, each 30ft 10in long by 10ft wide, with a carrying capacity of eighty-nine passengers and crew. These boats had a total capacity of 1,602 people. In addition, there

The *Empress of Britain* on her first arrival in Liverpool.

RIGHT
On her trials on 8 April 1931.

were six 25ft lifeboats capable of carrying a further 276 persons. There were also two 30ft motor lifeboats, each equipped with a 34hp paraffin engine and a self-contained wireless room. These boats had a speed of 8 knots, a range of 100 nautical miles and could carry forty-four people. The emergency fleet could, therefore, carry a total of 1,966 people while the ship's total complement was 1,909 people. Apart from this fleet of emergency boats, *Empress of Britain* was also provided with rafts that could carry 500 people.

Large crowds, both onshore and on the ship, watched as she was berthed in the dry dock at Liverpool, after her successful sea trials.

The steam turbines that drove the four propellers of the *Empress of Britain* developed 62,500shp and maintained a normal speed of 24 knots. For cruising, it was planned that the two outboard propellers would be removed as sufficient speed would be achieved by the use of the two inboard propellers alone: the two inboard engines developing twice the power of the outboard engines. Should an increase of speed above the normal be found necessary, an overload power was available to a maximum limit of 66,500shp, if the weather conditions were favourable. The dimensions of the turbine gearing of the *Empress of Britain* give some indication of the immense size of her machinery. The main gear wheel of each inboard engine was of 14ft 6in diameter,

with a width across the working face of 4ft 8in. The outboard wheels were 11ft 3⅛in in diameter, all gear teeth having been cut diagonally by special machines. The inboard turbines revolved at 1,365 revolutions per minute, and the outboard screw engines at 1,795 revolutions per minute. The propellers, cast in solid bronze, were enormous; each inboard propeller was 19ft 3in in diameter, weighed 25 tons and turned at 150rpm. The outboard propellers were 24ft in diameter and turned at 200rpm. Each propeller was so perfectly balanced that the pressure of a finger could rotate it.

The main steam-generating installation comprised eight Yarrow water-tube boilers, and one water-tube boiler of the Johnson type. There were also two smaller, auxiliary boilers. All were fired by oil fuel, which was sprayed in under pressure and supplied with a blast of pre-heated air to ensure combustion. Each of the Yarrow boilers was approximately 23ft long, 26ft high and 26ft wide. Six of these boilers were accommodated in an after boiler room and discharged fumes into the middle funnel. The remaining boilers were placed below the forward funnel, in the forward boiler room. There was a total length of over 100 miles of boiler tubing.

The requirements of the *Empress of Britain* for electricity were similar to those of a small town. The main generating plant comprised four diesel-driven 450 kilowatts generators that were housed in a special engine room. In addition, there were two steam-driven turbo-generators of 800 kilowatts each in the forward engine room, and a number of emergency generating sets and electric batteries. The demands on the electricity supply system were heavy, for not only were the lighting, heating and cooking dependent upon it, but also the auxiliary machinery. Five passenger lifts and seven other lifts were electrically operated, as were the winches, deck cranes, fans, laundry and various machinery. There were 407 electric motors aboard for different purposes, totalling 5,720hp.

At her bows on A Deck there were two anchors housed in recesses let into the hull. These weighed, with a third bower anchor, over 27 tons. Aft of these was a cargo hatch, with a steel cover. The hollow steel foremast towered 160ft above the Promenade Deck and, at heights of 80ft and 130ft respectively, were the lookout stations. The lower station was reached by a steel ladder inside the mast, and an external ladder linked the two stations.

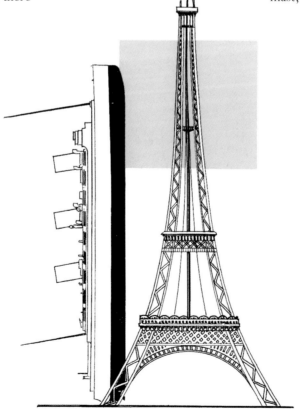

The Eiffel Tower is 984ft high. The *Empress of Britain* is 757ft long.

ART DECO MASTERPIECE

Her rooms are so spacious, so much like fine homes in their appointments and decorations, that they cease to be cabins or staterooms, but are real apartments on board ship. Seventy percent of these apartments have private baths. All of them have outside light and air. There are no 'inside' rooms. Instead of the old type Promenade Deck, the Empress of Britain *has a Lounge Deck. Inboard from this sweeping, spacious deck is a succession of brilliant rooms. Each decorated by a great artist. Each provides its own setting for gay social life. In her decorations, her speed, her comforts, her gaiety, she is truly a ship for the moderns, but particularly for those moderns who still think space is preferable to crowds. Her lavish dedication of space to a highly restricted passenger-list is probably the most astonishing development in the ocean-going world.*

Canadian Pacific brochure of 1931,
describing the first-class accommodation.

The *Empress of Britain* was designed to carry passengers in three classes: 465 in first class, 260 in tourist class and 470 in third class. However, as one might expect, her first-class passengers had more space per person than aboard any other ship then afloat. She was, to all intents, a first-class liner. By comparison, the 'Duchess' liners of just over 20,000grt and 600ft in length carried a total of 1,559 passengers in three classes whereas the *Empress of Britain*, at 42,348grt and 760ft length, carried a total of just 1,195 passengers. The larger part of the six decks of *Empress of Britain*, the Sun Deck, Lounge Deck, A, B, C and D Decks and an aft section of E Deck, were devoted to passenger accommodation and public rooms. First-class passengers had cabins, quite a large number of which were convertible into multi-roomed suites on the Sun Deck and in the central sections of A, B and C Decks. The entire length of the Lounge Deck was devoted to first-class public rooms (seven in all), the enclosed first-class promenades, and the after promenade deck. The promenade along either side of the boat deck, or the Sun Deck as it was known, was also reserved for the use of first-class passengers.

The public rooms for the tourist-class passengers were located aft on A and B Decks, while their cabin accommodation was aft on C, D and E Decks. Third-class passengers had a Lounge and some open deck space forward on A Deck and cabin accommodation forward on C, D and E Decks. There were also a group of twenty-one portable cabins, for up to sixty-eight people, forward on F Deck. If necessary, these cabins could be dismantled and the space used for the storage of cargo instead. The Dining Rooms for all three classes were on D Deck, the large first-class Dining Room in the centre, aft of which was the kitchen that served both this room and the tourist Dining Room, which was further aft. A separate kitchen served the third-class Dining Room, which was located forward of the casing of the forward funnel. Aft, on F Deck, was located the first-class Olympian Pool, gymnasium and Turkish bath.

While there was no doubt that any transatlantic liner devoting the larger part of its accommodation to the comfort of its first-class passengers was designed with the utmost care. However, the designers of the *Empress of Britain* had to also take into consideration the fact that the ship would spend up to four months of each year on a cruise around the world. (Most other transatlantic liners, no matter how grand, were not designed with this dual role in mind.) Her public rooms and cabins had to both look and feel comfortable and attractive whether she was battling her way across a stormy North Atlantic, or steaming serenely through the South China Seas. Nevertheless, the *Empress of Britain*, although the most modern of liners regarding her construction and internal fittings, met criticism from some quarters in that she presented an unusual combination of both the height of modernity and what was regarded as being staid traditionalism, internally, as well as with regard to her exterior profile. However, *The Shipbuilder and Marine Engine-Builder*, in their special edition to mark the entry into service of the liner, commented: 'Rarely, if ever, have such luxurious comfort and beauty in the passenger accommodation of the *Empress of Britain* been surpassed, either afloat or ashore.' In decorating the liner the underlying thought of Canadian Pacific had been the provision of as much variety and interest as was consistent with good taste. The company allocated £250,000 to decorate and furnish the public rooms but, instead of giving the job to the usual decorative architects they employed, Canadian Pacific commissioned Britain's best-known artists; each one being assigned to design the decorative scheme for a different room. They were allowed a fairly free hand with regard to their designs, the only limitation being that they should combine simplicity with dignity. While not having given their usual decorative architects, P.A. Staynes and A.H. Jones, the opportunity to work on the main public spaces, they were assigned perhaps an even more difficult task: the co-ordinating of the work of the diverse group of artists. Messrs Staynes and Jones were required to design the entrance foyer, the stairways and corridors all in an attempt to create a feeling of unity as the passengers moved from one space to another. They were also responsible for the designs of the Writing and Card Rooms, the Olympian Pool and the de luxe and special suites.

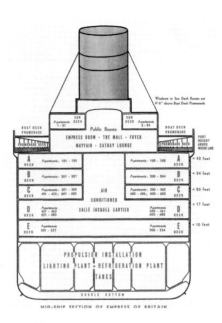

Mid-ship section of the *Empress of Britain*.

At the forward end of the impressive suite of first-class public rooms on the Lounge Deck was the Empress Room, otherwise known as the ballroom. This room was 40ft from forward to aft and 70ft wide. Its simple classical style was decorated to a design by the noted artist, Sir John Lavery, R.A. Silvered pilasters with gold capitals relieved the panelled walls, and the colours used throughout the room were mainly coral pink and blue. The aft wall of the room was panelled in mirror, while at strategic points around the room there were silvered pedestals surmounted by rose-coloured ostrich plumes. The orchestra stage was hung with draperies of turquoise and rose while the dance floor, of polished Austrian oak, was surrounded by chairs covered in blue and beige fabric, these being arranged around tables, the bases of which were silvered dolphin shapes. The central part of the ceiling over the dance floor was a dome: painted deep blue, it was decorated with stars arranged as they had appeared in the night sky on the day that the ship was launched. It was a very feminine room, the décor and clever lighting arrangement created in order to enhance the elegant evening gowns that would usually be worn in the room. This was, however, a dual-purpose room: it could be used as a cinema. At the forward end of the

OPPOSITE

With the *Empress of Britain* comes the new 'era of residence' aboard ship. Her de luxe apartments, without exaggeration, can be said to offer the exquisite appointments and facilities of Park Avenue, with the seclusion of Park Lane. Each principal apartment consists of a spacious living room, a cheery Sun Verandah, a charming double bedroom (shown here), an unusually large bathroom as well as a servant's room and convenient, ample luggage room. Each makes possible as complete, secluded and delightful life as in the finest private homes.

OVERLEAF

THE EMPRESS ROOM BY SIR JOHN LAVERY, R.A.

Here, one of Britain's foremost artists has wrought a setting keyed to rhythm and carnival. Delicate corals, blues and silvers flow down, in restrained design, to meet the gleaming parquet floor. They re-echo in the delightful expanse of mirrored walls. Here, one dances away the magic of ocean nights. One plays under a canopy of sky which reproduces the heavens at the time of the liner's launching. One watches divertissements presented from a night-club stage. This room is the centre of indoor gaiety.

To light the ship requires 17,000 electric lamps. The generating plant is capable of lighting a town the size of Scarborough.

The Knickerbocker Bar in use.

THE MALL BY P.A. STAYNES AND A.H. JONES.

Finding they can ascend the main staircase five abreast is only one method whereby passengers may readily feel the magnificent spaciousness of the *Empress of Britain*. Thus they ascend to The Mall. Here, Mr Staynes and Mr Jones have fashioned a long inner promenade of moulded oak, brilliantly illuminated by unique crystal pendants. With its far-reaching vistas and its accessibility to every part of the Lounge Deck, The Mall naturally becomes the ideal rendezvous in which to decide the activities of the day or evening.

room there was a cinema-operating room, fitted with the most modern type of sound-film (or in those days 'talkie') equipment.

Moving aft from the ballroom, on either side of the forward funnel casing, were spaces designated as The Mall, and these led into the vast Main Foyer. The Mall and Foyer combined were in fact one of the largest public spaces aboard the ship, being 165ft in length. The main staircase was at the forward end of the Foyer, and opposite was the shop, which was decorated with illuminated glass turrets.

On the starboard side of the central funnel casing was the Writing Room, and this was decorated in what was described as being 'a free adaptation of the Georgian period.' Opposite the Writing Room, on the port side, was one of the more remarkably decorated rooms aboard the ship, the Knickerbocker Bar. This was a small cocktail bar, with seating for a little over twenty people, and panelled in sycamore. What made the room so remarkable was the fact that the inventive cartoonist, W. Heath Robinson, was responsible for the decoration of the room. A humorous mural, of his creation, purporting to show the history of the cocktail, encircled the room. The ceiling also had several circular panels that showed his whimsical characters looking down and a fragile-looking aircraft flying overhead.

Located in the space between the second and third funnel casings was the Mayfair Lounge, which was in effect the main Lounge. While opulent and richly decorated, it was somewhat conventional in styling, with Sir Charles Allom being responsible for the decor. *The Shipbuilder and Marine*

The international Mr Robinson, who is by way of being one of the world's most inventive humorists, has been allowed free rein in the Knickerbocker Bar. His hilarious mural 'Legend of the Cocktail' portrays that beverage in fantastic evolution… revealing the infinite variety of his entertaining skill as applied to that most subtle of creations. With colourful wealth of whimsical imagery, his frolicsome fancies form a fine fantastic setting for the cocktail's joyous errand to edge the appetite and whet the wit.

W. Heath Robinson creating his masterpiece 'Legend of the Cocktail'.

MAYFAIR BY CHARLES ALLOM

Mayfair, on the Lounge Deck, is the name of the great central salon of the *Empress of Britain*.
Sir Charles Allom has utilised the grand spaces of this room to create a brilliant central setting,
bordered by restful vistas and large-windowed bays. The decorative motif is Renaissance.
Rich walnut panelling is picked out in silver. Marble pilasters are ornamented in bronze.
The tympanum sunburst is a glory of simplified modern conception. In this vast room,
one has the feeling of a delightful and sparkling society – Mayfair.

Engine-Builder wrote about it thus: 'Created in noble and dignified proportions. The main architectural features are inspired by the ancient Temple of Minerva.' The walls were panelled in a richly grained walnut with silver enrichments; the columns and pilasters were of green Scagliola marble enriched with fine bronze ornamentation, while the mantelpiece, and the top of the large octagonal table in the centre of the room, was in Scagliola Verdite. The domed ceiling over the centre section of the room was of amber glass panels: each panel having a golden sunray centre, while the intersecting panels had the signs of the zodiac. The room was furnished with large settees and armchairs in subdued colours; fine silk damask was used for the curtains and other draperies. The floor, of parquetry in Austrian oak, was covered with rich carpets reproduced from an antique Polish design of the sixteenth century and manufactured in Persia; real gold wire was used for the gold parts of the design.

While the Mayfair Lounge may have represented the traditional face of the *Empress of Britain*, the Smoking Room, or Cathay Lounge, was undoubtedly the face of modernity. This was the most strikingly decorated room aboard the ship (and indeed, probably the most strikingly original room ever created for a British ocean liner), the design being created by Mr Edmund Dulac. In a lavishly illustrated brochure to mark the liner's entry into service, it stated: 'From the vivid modern brush of this artist comes the suave dignity of the Cathay Lounge. This setting replaces, in effect, those forbidding "ship smoke-rooms" of yesterday. All that is brilliant and vigorous in the colour of the ancient Far East, Mr Dulac has portrayed through the refinements of his conception. A ceiling of shimmering silver balances a goldengrated parquet. All are held in calm restraint through the use of choice, natural woods and simple Chinese lacquer.' The walls of this remarkable and beautiful room were panelled in grey ash, with ornamental

ABOVE & BELOW

Cocktail Hour in the Cathay Lounge.

ABOVE

CATHAY LOUNGE BY EDMUND DULAC

From the vivid modern brush of this artist, the *Arabian Nights* genius of the generation, comes the suave dignity of the Cathay Lounge. This setting replaces, in effect, those forbidding 'ship smoke-rooms' of yesterday. All that is brilliant and vigorous in the colour of the ancient Far East, Mr Dulac has portrayed through the refinements of his conception. A ceiling of shimmering silver balances a golden-toned parquet. The bar and fireplace are of translucent glass. All are held in calm restraint through the use of choice, natural woods and simple Chinese lacquer. In such a setting the serious globe-trotters aboard the *Empress of Britain* gather in conversational exchange.

decorations in red and black lacquer. Lights of a special design in moulded glass were fitted to the walls and pillars, and a special feature was the glass fireplace, in which mirrors of peach, gold, green and black were used. To either side of the fireplace were two huge red lacquer Chinese vases. The floor was of inlaid Macassar ebony and oak in a trellis pattern, and the furniture, which was specially designed for the room, was in red and black lacquer ornamented in pale gold and covered in coral-coloured fabric of a Chinese design.

The first-class Dining Room, or Salle Jacques Cartier to give its correct name, occupied the full width of the ship, was over 120ft in length and its centre section was two decks in height. The room, which Canadian Pacific advertised as being the largest afloat without supporting pillars, was able to accommodate 452 diners. The design of the room was the responsibility of Frank Brangwyn, R.A., and he painted two large decorative panels that covered the walls at either end of the room, depicting incidents in the life of the French explorer of the St Lawrence River, Jacques Cartier. Mr Brangwyn also created other murals of human figures as well as fruit and flowers, and he designed the pattern of the rubber-based composition that cover the floor as well as the light-oak chairs and tables used in the room. The walls of the room were panelled in light oak, with oak beams dividing the panelled ceiling. A tall octagonal buffet, with three tiers of gold mirrors that were lit at the apex, made a striking centrepiece to the room. Either side of the entrance to the Dining Room were two private rooms that could be opened up and thus be incorporated into the main room.

SALLE JACQUES CARTIER BY FRANK BRANGWYN, R.A.

LEFT
Dining in the Salle Jacques Cartier.

OPPOSITE
So spacious is this Dining Room with its adjacent private Dining Rooms that each table affords the secluded atmosphere at home. Mr Brangwyn, famous for his mastery of ship traditions, has wrought them into this setting with his own inimitable imagery. His spreading frescoes, fore and aft, unfold a full tableau of the Earth's bounties... delightful and appropriate background for a metropolitan cuisine such as the *Empress of Britain*'s. And whenever one's whim is fresh caviar from the intriguing cold buffet in the room's centre... or Lobster Thermidor from the hot-plate of the nearby serving table... each dish appears attended by that ready graciousness which is true of all Canadian Pacific Service.

Everything is cooked by electricity except grilled orders – for experience shows that nothing suits your steak like a charcoal fire.

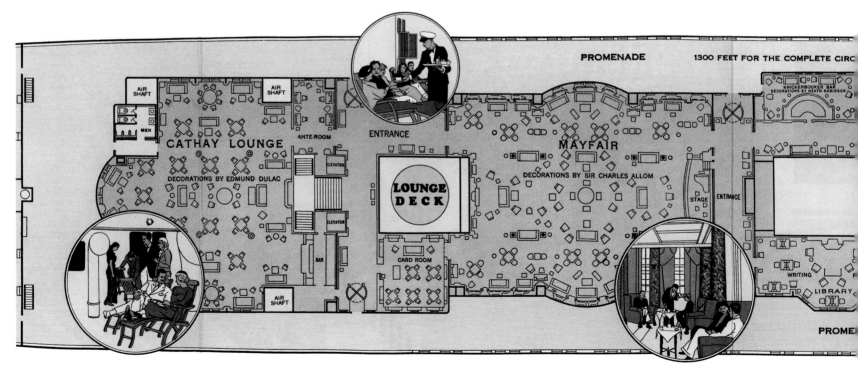

Down on F Deck, under a full-glass ceiling, was the 40ft x 20ft Olympian Pool. It was the largest pool in any vessel then afloat. Eight fluted turquoise glass and mosaic columns supported the illuminated ceiling, forming a colonnade around the pool. Water spouted from a large turtle that was carved from Portland stone and inlaid with blue mosaic, at the after end of the pool. On both sides of the pool were changing facilities; to the port side was a fully equipped gymnasium and on starboard, Turkish baths. At the forward end was a small café.

RIGHT & FOLLOWING SPREAD

OLYMPIAN POOL

Under a full glass ceiling, which gleams like the brilliant warmth of the Adriatic sunshine, this exquisite setting is a veritable Lido in activity. Water spouts into the enormous swimming pool from a sea turtle of terrazzo glass. Hidden under the surface, lights pick up the sparkle of its plunge. A terraced café borders the pool's forward end – spectators' galleries command its sides – and the whole is set amid delicate glass mosaics and adroitly carved teak. Turkish and electric baths, as well as a fully equipped gymnasium, adjoin the Pool to form a complete locale for gay exercise and invigorating relaxation aboard the *Empress of Britain*.

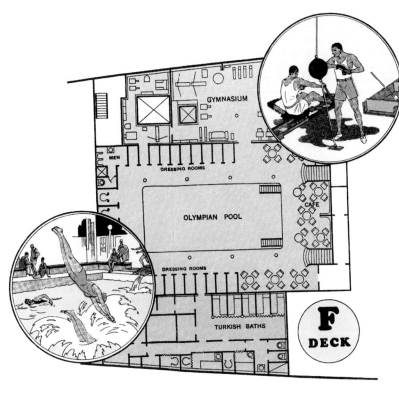

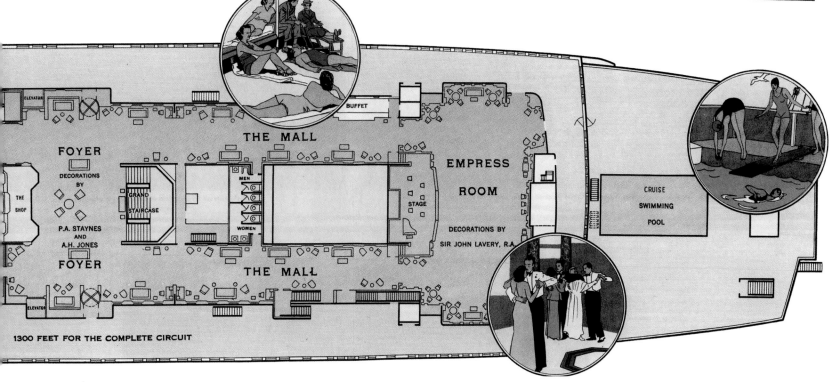

1300 FEET FOR THE COMPLETE CIRCUIT

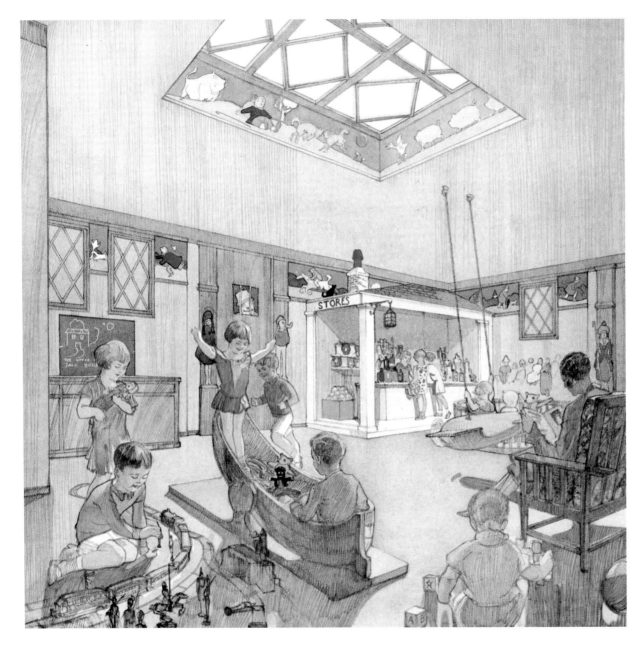

CHILDREN'S PLAYROOM BY W. HEATH ROBINSON

Here, Mr Heath Robinson shows he can call forth a smile from ages three to six as well as from thirty to sixty. In the playroom, he has transplanted nursery-rhyme heroes and heroines into wall decorations… each with a touch that sometimes reminds you of animal crackers and sometimes of soap bubbles. Then, too, very serious 'shopping-like-mother' can take place at the miniature stores. And there's a toy aeroplane that swishes you through the air but still is very safe. And there's a rocking-boat, and trains, and dolls, and blocks, and a black-board – and a governess attendant who knows just what to do when youngsters are exacting, and just what to do when they're lovable.

A playroom for children was located up on the Sun Deck, its panelled walls being covered in scenes from fairy stories by Heath Robinson. Aft on this deck was a full-size tennis court, either side of which were galleries for the spectators. Seeing their passengers as a potentially athletic group, a regulation-size squash court was located on B Deck.

With the *Empress of Britain* came what Canadian Pacific's advertising department referred to as 'a new era of "Residence aboard ship."' In a lavish 1932-produced brochure they went on to describe the first-class accommodations thus: 'In nothing is the exceptional spaciousness of the ship – giving more cubic space per first-class passenger than any other ship

DE LUXE APARTMENTS

The living rooms of these de luxe apartments well epitomise the liner's chic residential atmosphere. Here, for example, as in the seclusion and convenience of one's own ménage, one may order a quiet luncheon or tea for twelve, or dine happily without asking the steward to rearrange the furniture. Or here, one may just relax in the luxury of a deep divan, gaze through the broad windows at the rhythm of the sparkling sea… and feel delightfully at home on the *Empress of Britain*.

afloat – demonstrated so much as in the generous provisions of the living quarters. These are truly called, not cabins or staterooms, but apartments. All these, of whatever kind, are outside ones, having either windows or portholes. You don't sleep in a berth, but in a real bed. You arrange your hair before a triple-mirrored dressing table and study your complete evening effect in a full-length wall mirror. You keep your clothes in wardrobes fitted with hangers and tie-racks and trees and things, and your toilet requisites in a wall cabinet. You can have all the little comfort-making gadgets – dressing lights, curling iron outfits, reading lights, bedside tables, telephones, call-bells, fans, heaters. You have steam heat

and ball-louvre pressure ventilation. Of the apartments, 75 per cent have either a beautifully fitted private bathroom, or shower and toilet. All have wood panelled walls, and perfect taste and comfort in decoration and furnishing. Ample provision is made for a wide range of moderately priced accommodation. This range comprises single and double apartments, there are also many de luxe double rooms and three kinds of private suites. In addition to these many adjoining apartments may be used "en suite."'

Of the three kinds of suites mentioned, each epitomised the seclusion of the residential atmosphere. Each consisted of an entrance hall, a double bedroom, a spacious living room, an unusually large bathroom and ample luggage room. The largest of these suites, made up of cabins 147-149-151 on port side and 144-146-148 on starboard, also included the ultimate luxury of what was described as a Sun Verandah; furnished with cane furniture this space had three large, floor to ceiling windows. The décor of the suites was varied in design, and much use was made of exotic woods such as Queensland maple, black bean, angelim, locust, Macassar ebony, figured Quebec ash and avodire as well as the more familiar mahogany, sycamore, ash and oak. One suite featured a mural decoration of deep red Chinese lacquer, with a carpet in soft shades of fawn and furniture in old-ivory lacquer. In the other first-class cabin accommodation again much use was made of more beautiful woods including satinwood, Australian silky oak,

Two types of double apartments are seen here. The top one (329) was the recessed type with private bath while the lower (253) was a double apartment with optional private bath.

A double de luxe apartment (10) on the Sports Deck.

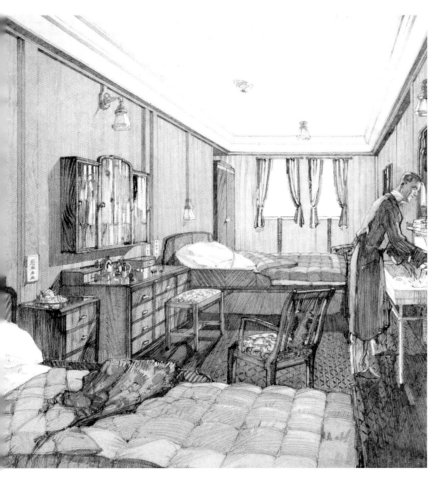

ONE ROOM APARTMENTS (DOUBLE).

Although of one room, these apartments for two have an atmosphere of liveability which only spacious and lovely appointments can give. Large bedsteads… charming dressing tables with roomy cabinet backs and triple-folding mirrors… cabinet for toilet requisites… a full-length wall mirror… elaborately equipped full size wardrobes for each passenger… besides easy chairs, armchairs, bedside tables… all these are more than mere conveniences because of the faultless taste in which they are designed and arranged. Such apartments, of course, each have private bathrooms adjoining.

RIGHT

These apartments have been ingeniously contrived and equipped so that their single occupants may be as far as possible a law unto themselves. Just as the apartments for two, these liveable rooms are furnished in perfect modern taste as well as with perfect modern convenience. Nothing is forgotten… outlets for electric fans and heaters, even for curling-irons… low-pressure steam heat under individual control… ball-louvre pressure ventilation for either warming or cooling the fresh air before it enters the apartment. Like all first-class apartments aboard the *Empress of Britain*, they are 'outside' with natural light and air… and charming to be alone in at home. And each has its private bathroom adjoining.

The *Empress of Britain*
has altogether 120 clocks, all
synchronised from chronometers on the bridge.

The New
EMPRESS OF BRITAIN

40,000 TONS

in service 1931, will make the Atlantic
crossing between Quebec and
Southampton - Cherbourg inside five
days. With elaborate sports - deck,
luxurious Public Rooms and
State - Rooms. The new White
Empress will introduce new standards
of comfort and pleasure afloat.

Speed - - - - 24 knots
Length - - - - 755 feet
Breadth - - - - 97½ feet

Designed for service on the St.
Lawrence seaway to and from Europe.

BELOW
Suites 163-165 had sitting rooms adjoining
the bedrooms.

Elevators serve all decks up to the Sports Deck. Even numbered apartments are on the starboard side of the ship – odd-numbered, on the port side.

The Smoking Room.

Canadian birds-eye maple, sapele and African and Burmese mahogany. There were also a large number of single berth cabins, several of which had communicating doors with either another single, or double cabin. Another refinement that highlighted the modernity of the new Empress was the telephone: she was the first vessel in which an international telephone service was available from passengers' cabins.

The tourist-class passengers had just three principal public rooms: the Smoking Room, Lounge and Dining Room. The Smoking Room was located aft, on A Deck. The room was panelled in limed and wax-polished oak. The main feature of the room was a marble fireplace that was surmounted by shaped mirrors. The room, which also contained a bar at its aft end, on the port side, was furnished with easy chairs and settees covered in tapestry of different designs and colours. Forward of this room, across the entrance hall, was the gymnasium. Immediately below the Smoking Room was the tourist-class Lounge. Again, much use was made of exotic woods in its decoration, with the walls being panelled in quartered sycamore that was divided by pilasters of Zebrano. The chairs and settees that furnished the room were

covered in various shades of orange and green. The central section of the floor of the room was laid with polished Austrian oak to form a dance floor. The tourist-class Dining Room was on D Deck, and occupied the full width of the ship. It had a seating capacity for 164 diners at tables for 2, 4 or 6. The walls of the room were panelled in French walnut and Zebrano, sunken pilasters divided the panels, and at the head of each pilaster was a glass decoration in the form of a cascade with a fan of plaster spreading out over the ceiling. This fan design was picked out in green and silver. The walnut chairs were upholstered in orange-coloured hide and, in the centre of the room were two buffets in walnut and fitted with mirrors. The tourist-class passengers were accommodated in two and four-berth cabins, a large number of which were outside through the use of the 'Bibby' principle. The lower beds in these cabins were of such a design that they were able to support the upper berths, and these upper berths were thus removable in order to make these cabins useable when the ship was employed on cruises. None of these cabins were provided with their own private bathrooms, but there were ample public bath and toilet facilities. There were open deck spaces and promenades on both sides and aft of the Smoking Room and Lounge.

The third-class passengers were accommodated in altogether simpler surroundings, albeit still attractive, at the forward end of the ship. There was a Lounge on A Deck, panelled in cherry wood and oak. The room also contained a bar and a shop. On B Deck there was what was referred to as an airing space, and from this there was access to a children's room. The dining saloon was on D Deck, and was served by its own kitchen. As with the other two classes, this Dining Room was the full width of the ship and could accommodate 234 people. The cabins were arranged for either two or four people and, while much simpler in style, nevertheless conformed to the high standards elsewhere throughout the ship. The cabins were panelled in plywood, which was painted in light shades, and hot and cold water was laid onto each one.

The captain was accommodated in a style similar to that of the passengers in first class, in a suite of rooms on the captain's bridge, forward of the Sports Deck. The staff captain and the navigating officers were on the deck below while the chief engineers and the other engineering officers were on the starboard side of B Deck; in a similar position on the deck below was accommodation for the junior engineers. Further crew accommodation

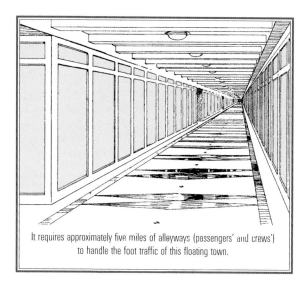

It requires approximately five miles of alleyways (passengers' and crews') to handle the foot traffic of this floating town.

was on C and D Decks, forward, and D Deck, aft. However, the majority of the crew were accommodated on E Deck.

The *Empress of Britain* was also fitted with an extensive hospital, on C Deck, as well as an isolation hospital, aft on A Deck.

It has been said that the seriousness with which Canadian Pacific undertook the task of decorating their new flagship was more French than British and, while it has been suggested that this was a gracious tribute to the Gallic heritage of Canada, there was one regrettable oversight. None of the on-board signage was in any other language than English!

Even though the *Empress of Britain* would not be sailing on the most prestigious of ocean liner routes, Europe to New York, she was, without any doubt, the equal of any of the grand ships of state that plied that route. Indeed, as the Prince of Wales had implied at his speech at her launching, she surpassed many of them. With her three imposing funnels and white hull and superstructure she imparted an air of both majesty and power while her interiors – a combination of genteel adaptations of period styles spiked with the hard-edged glamour of the then highly fashionable 'art-deco' – came together to make the *Empress of Britain* the most stylish and highly individual liner ever built for a British company. Also, at 42,348grt, she was the largest liner to ply between any two ports of the British Empire.

Dressed in flags, outward bound past Cowes, Isle of Wight.

CROSSINGS AND CRUISING

In one season, without dispute, the Empress became the travel sensation of the world – partly because of her speed, partly because of her beauty. To this there is testimony to be found in her first season's passenger list, which is almost a 'Who's Who' of the great ones of the earth. The beauty of her external lines, spick and span and lovely in white paint, crowds the deck-rails of other ships she passes in mid-ocean, or draws admiring crowds to the dock when she steams majestically up Southampton Water or round the Isle d'Orleans, approaching Quebec. This admiration is heightened when you are on board, for there the beauty of the ship is doubly manifest. It can be truly said that with the Empress of Britain *a new era in passenger travel began.*

Canadian Pacific brochure, 1932.

As the new liner gleamed in the late spring sunshine at her Southampton berth, the gloom of the Depression weighed ever more heavily upon the country. Many of the men who had helped create her now joined the ranks of the jobless, and the figure of Britain's unemployed reached 2,648,000.

On 13 May 1931, just two weeks before the *Empress of Britain* was due to depart Southampton on her maiden voyage, an inaugural lunch was held in the Salle Jacques Cartier. The European Manager of Canadian Pacific, Sir George McLaren Brown, drew the guests' attention to the fact that the exceptional cruising speed of the new liner, which would be around 24 knots, would reduce the open sea passage to no more than 3½ days and, as a consequence, bring the Orient closer. Working in conjunction with the new and fast *Empress of Japan*, the *Empress of Britain* would help save at least two days between London and Yokohama. Sir George's audience were amused when he assured them that it would be cheaper for them to live aboard the new Empress each winter as she cruised the world, rather than to remain at home.

As those two weeks ticked by the *Empress of Britain* was made ready for her first voyage across the Atlantic to Canada. Then the day arrived, and shortly before the ship was due to sail, a surprise visitor, the Prince of Wales, was hurried aboard. Having performed the naming ceremony he was anxious to see the ship depart on her first voyage – a decision he'd made only the night before! While only a small handful of senior people at Canadian Pacific were advised of the Prince's imminent arrival, somehow word got out and spread amongst the crowd on the dockside. The Prince had flown down to Southampton from Hendon aerodrome in his own Puss Moth bi-plane, and having announced that he didn't want his visit to disrupt the scheduled departure of the ship, he rushed around in just half-an-hour, seeing as much as he could. As he left the ship the Prince said to Captain Latta: 'My only regret is that I am not sailing too!' Despite his good intentions, the visit of the Prince did delay the departure, albeit briefly, but at 1.12 p.m. the majestic new liner eased away from her berth. The Prince of Wales, meanwhile, had crossed to Hythe by speedboat, and there he had boarded the Imperial Airways flying boat *Satyrus*. Taking over the controls himself, the Prince piloted the aircraft out towards the sea, then he turned and flew low over the *Empress of Britain*, dipping the plane's wings in salute. The maiden voyage had begun, and in high style!

It has been stated that the maiden voyage of the ship set the tone for her entire career: it was a complete and apparently effortless triumph. On the day she departed Southampton the *Daily Express* announced: 'An event of Imperial moment takes place today. The *Empress of Britain* sails on her maiden voyage from Southampton to Canada. The same vision and faith that flung the railways across Canada from ocean to ocean in superb confidence that settlers and trade would follow have inspired this magnificent vessel. The skill and experience of British shipwrights have built her. The finest ship on all the seas, she is also vibrant proof of what Canada and Britain working together can achieve.'

Initially, Canadian Pacific had announced that the *Empress of Britain* would depart on her maiden voyage in late June, arriving in Canada towards the end of the month. Then the date was brought forward, with the ship arriving in Canada on 1 June. Sadly, this had an effect on the number of passengers booking on that first voyage and, as a consequence, she sailed with just a handful of passengers: 201 in first class, 86 in tourist and 63 in third. Adding an additional aura of glamour to the crossing was the presence of Douglas Fairbanks and Mary Pickford, at the time two of Hollywood's greatest motion picture stars. Viscount Rothermere, the proprietor of the *Daily Mail*, was also aboard, and he reported in most favourable terms about the ship, describing her as 'the finest vessel ever launched.' Mr C.H.J. Snider, the news editor of the *Toronto Evening Telegram*, who was also aboard and sending daily reports to his paper, enthused: 'A bold Canadian bid for a topmost seat in the sun of shipping supremacy.' Such enthusiasm helped heighten the intense anticipation that was already felt by many people in Canada. The progress of the construction and fitting out of the ship had been regularly reported in their newspapers from the very beginning.

For this first voyage the *Empress of Britain* had a smooth crossing, encountering only moderate breezes and a slight to moderate sea. As she neared Quebec on 1 June, the crowd that had gathered to greet the new liner had swelled to over 100,000. Shortly before 10.00 p.m. the *Empress of Britain* was securely alongside, having completed a record crossing in 5 days, 13 hours and 25 minutes (as reported in the *Montreal Gazette*).

The *Empress of Britain* at San Francisco.

Two 18in high intensity searchlights are installed as additional navigational aids on the Captain's bridge.

ABOVE LEFT

As the new liner gleamed in the late spring sunshine at her Southampton berth, the gloom of the Depression weighed ever more heavily upon the country.

OPPOSITE

The *Empress of Britain* at Quebec after her maiden voyage.

FAR LEFT

Famous passengers included Douglas Fairbanks and Mary Pickford…

LEFT

…and Edgar Wallace.

OVERLEAF

She left Southampton on 2 September 1939, her portholes covered and a blackout imposed. War was declared as she sailed for Quebec.

However, the ship had taken the slightly longer route and, when the seasonal danger of icebergs had passed, she would be taken through the strait between Labrador and Newfoundland. Mr E.W. Beatty, president and chairman of Canadian Pacific, who had been aboard for the voyage, confidently announced that the ship would be able to make the passage from Cherbourg to Quebec in just four-and-a-half days. Naturally, the press had wanted to interview Douglas Fairbanks and Mary Pickford once the Empress had docked. Mr Fairbanks said that he had found just two faults in the voyage. One, it was too short because of the many attractions the ship offered; and two, those same attractions robbed one of the sense of being on an ocean voyage.

The *Empress of Britain* remained at Quebec for three days and during this time was opened to the public. Over 15,000 visitors, each paying 25 cents, made their way through the impressive array of public rooms. The money that was raised was given to charity. On 2 June a gala banquet was held aboard, with the Prime Minister of Canada, the Premier of Quebec and the Lieutenant-Governors of Quebec, New Brunswick and Prince Edward Island as principal guests. Other guests from the world of business and politics as well as society helped fill the beautiful Salle Jacques Cartier. During the banquet it was announced that Captain Latta had been appointed as Commodore of the Canadian Pacific fleet.

At 4.30 p.m. on Saturday 6 June the *Empress of Britain* cast off from her berth at Quebec for her return voyage to Southampton. Aboard were 238 first-class passengers and 295 divided between tourist and third classes. Once again a crowd of several thousand had gathered to watch her depart. After 4 days, 9 hours and 20 minutes the liner arrived at Cherbourg, having set a new record for the Quebec–Cherbourg crossing. During the remainder of that summer the *Empress of Britain* made sixteen further Atlantic crossings and, during this time, proved to be both very reliable and efficient, her outward and return voyages being almost identical in crossing times. Several times she broke her own records, and there were those journalists that drew comparisons between her crossings and those of the Blue Riband-holding liner *Europa*, and declared that the *Empress of Britain* was rightly the holder of the award. However, the Blue Riband was only ever awarded to liners on the New York service: thus denying the Empress this ultimate accolade. With such reliability it was proved that the *Empress of Britain* could provide a fortnightly service. It was not until August – three months after she had entered service – that Canadian Pacific got the opportunity to see how their new flagship could deal with really bad weather. On 25 August, after having steaming off the French coast for 8 hours, the gale force winds and heavy seas prohibiting the liner from entering Cherbourg harbour to disembark 133 passengers, the attempt was abandoned and she steamed for Southampton. Her passengers, still in bed in those early hours, were apparently blissfully unaware of the storm raging outside, so well did the ship ride the heavy seas.

Although not employed on the prestigious Atlantic route to New York, the *Empress of Britain* was continually in the news, not only with her record-breaking crossing times but also with the glamorous personalities that chose to sail aboard. In that first season, as well as Douglas Fairbanks and Mary Pickford,

Charming fellow guests for your World Cruise.

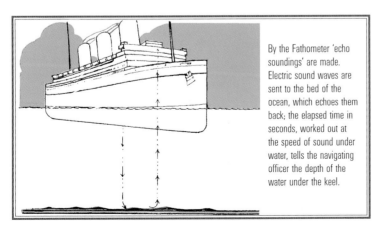

By the Fathometer 'echo soundings' are made. Electric sound waves are sent to the bed of the ocean, which echoes them back; the elapsed time in seconds, worked out at the speed of sound under water, tells the navigating officer the depth of the water under the keel.

who were aboard for the maiden voyage, the movie star Jeanette MacDonald also sailed on the ship, as did the writers P.G. Wodehouse and Edgar Wallace, Mr Wallace later writing that the Empress was: 'the grandest ship on the ocean.' The publicists Rafael Sabatini, Lord Rothermere, Lord Beaverbrook and Lord Castlerosse were also aboard the ship during that first season and, on her 27 June departure from Quebec, the Maharajah and Maharani of Sind and their daughters, the Princesses Beryl, Ruby and Diamond, added a particularly exotic glamour to the first-class passenger list. The *Empress of Britain* really appeared to have made her mark as one of the most prestigious liners, even earning herself the reputation as 'Mayfair afloat'. This, however, did not translate into numbers of passengers, for when one looked at the hard facts,

She entered dry dock in preparation for her World Cruise. Two propellers were removed and her aft engine room closed down. Cabins and public spaces were converted and she was readied for 128 days around the world.

the actual numbers of passengers carried was rather disappointing, albeit that they were largely the cream of society! In first class she had carried just 2,113 passengers westbound and 1,687 eastbound; in tourist class there had been 2,216 westbound and 1,707 eastbound, and in third class 562 westbound and 1,302 eastbound. In that first season, on average, the ship had sailed at less than half full on each voyage.

In November, the *Empress of Britain* entered Southampton's floating dry dock in preparation for her first World Cruise. The major part of the work was the removal of her two outer propellers, her after engine room being closed down because there was no need for her high speed during the 128-day cruise.

While Canadian Pacific were already experienced in the operation of World Cruises, the nearly four-month-long cruise to be operated by their largest and most luxurious ship, and the most prestigious liner in the world to operate such a cruise, was a difficult task to organise, even under the best of circumstances, so at the height of the Depression it became even more difficult. A lavish sixty-four-page brochure advertising the cruise was issued, with fares set at a minimum of $2,000 (most of her passengers being expected to come from the United States). The minimum fare for British passengers was 417 guineas. Not only did Canadian Pacific have the effects of the Depression to contend with when trying to sell this truly fabulous voyage, there was also the competition from other steamship lines that were sending their liners on an annual cruise around the world: Cunard with their very popular *Franconia*, the Red Star Line *Belgenland* and the Hamburg–Amerika Line *Resolute*. They were all handsome and well-appointed ships but none came close to the grand-luxe of the Empress. Her third-class accommodation, with the exception of thirty-four cabins, forward, on D Deck, was closed off, and those remaining cabins were rearranged to accommodate just one or two persons. In general, these cabins were made available to the servants who would be travelling with their masters or mistresses on the cruise. Likewise, the tourist-class cabins had their upper berths removed, turning them into either single or double cabins. The tourist Smoking Room was retained but the tourist Lounge became the cruise office for the arranging of the often-extensive overland

The price list for the 1932/33 World Cruise. Prices ranged from $2,250 per person for a berth in outside cabin 656 on D Deck, to $20,000 in one of the suites (with bedroom, sitting room, bath, baggage room and reception hall) for two persons. 129 days, 23 countries, 81 ports and places.

excursions that were planned, and the tourist Dining Room was turned into the staff Dining Room. Once in the warmer latitudes, forward on the Lounge Deck, in the space normally taken by No.2 cargo hatch, a swimming pool would be installed. The cruise was to cover 29,495 miles, and would include calls at eighty-one ports in twenty-three countries.

On 21 November the *Empress of Britain* sailed from Southampton on the first leg of the World Cruise, an Atlantic crossing for her first call at New York – where the majority of the passengers for the cruise would board. That final week of November 1931 was quite a special one for New York; on 23 November the city had already given a splendid welcome to the new Furness Bermuda Line ship, *Monarch of Bermuda*. Then, on 27 November, the

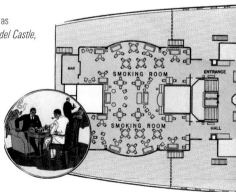

Empress of Britain arrived and, although now a few months old, the glamorous Empress rather outshone the brand new, and very smart 'Monarch'. During her stay in New York the *Empress of Britain* naturally generated a great deal of interest, and much of this was focussed on her striking interior. In an interview with Captain Latta, when this aspect of his ship was mentioned, he replied: 'She's a real ship, and that's my idea of it, not the decorations and the rest. I mean the ship.'

On the morning of Saturday 3 December, 332 passengers, plus a large crowd of friends, relatives and interested spectators, made their way to Pier 62. One passenger, who caught the attention of the press reporters and spectators alike, was the heiress Barbara Hutton, who was taking the cruise with her mother. By noon all visitors were ashore and lining the pier; multi-coloured streamers cascaded down the side of the *Empress of Britain* as she slowly backed into the Hudson River, turned, and headed towards her first port of call, Funchal, Madeira. From there she would continue to Gibraltar and Algiers, and then Monaco. It was there that European passengers, mostly British, who had not wished to endure two mid-winter Atlantic crossings – regardless of the superior sea-keeping qualities of the Empress – would board the ship. Then, at 1.00 a.m. on 17 December, with just over 400 passengers aboard, the *Empress of Britai*n set sail for Naples and then Athens. A highlight of the cruise for many passengers was the opportunity to spend Christmas in the Holy Land, with the ship arriving in the early morning of Christmas Eve in Haifa. All-inclusive in the cruise fare were opportunities to visit Jerusalem, Bethlehem and the Mount of Olives. The passengers taking advantage of this extended side trip rejoined the ship on 1 January 1932 in Suez. Having left the Red Sea, the *Empress of Britain*

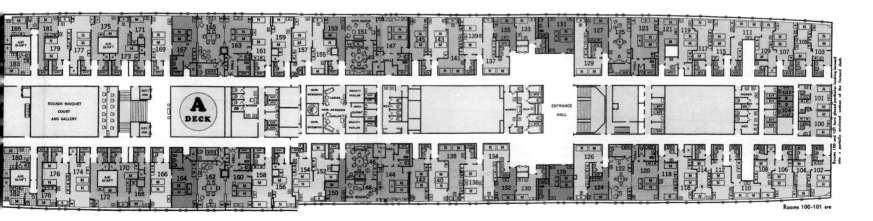

Rooms 100-101 are

OPPOSITE
Transiting the Suez Canal.

RIGHT
Hong Kong – one of the most beautiful
harbours in the world.

BELOW RIGHT
The *Empress of Britain* sails out of Southampton
on the first leg of a World Cruise.

steamed across the Indian Ocean to Bombay, anchoring in the harbour there on 7 January, and remaining until the evening of 15 Janury. The lengthy stay allowed passengers to travel on quite extended trips, and upon disembarking the Empress's tenders, there were four trains waiting to take passengers on their tours. Having left India, the *Empress of Britain* continued on to Colombo for a four-day stay, then on to Padang in Sumatra and Batavia on Java before arriving in Singapore on 1 February. Then she steamed on up towards Bangkok and then on to Manila. The scheduled call at Shanghai had to be cancelled due to the fighting that was happening around the city so instead the passengers were given an extended stay in Hong Kong. After the five-day stay in the British colony, the Empress headed up to Chinwangtao, where her passengers were able to take a five-day trip to Peking. Ten days were spent cruising around Japan, with calls at Beppu, Kobe and Yokohama,

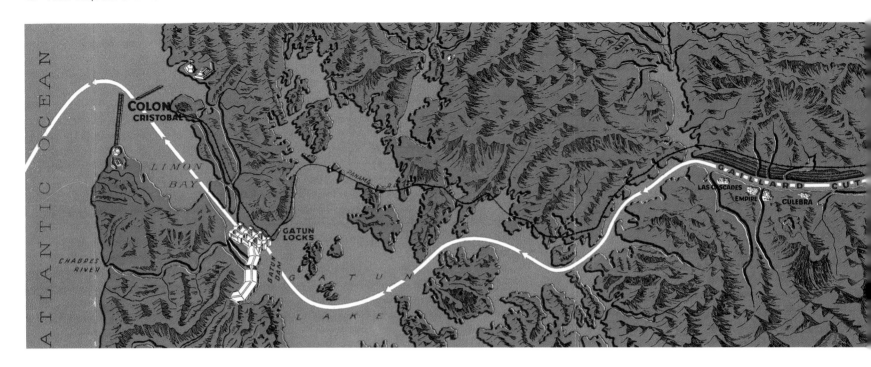

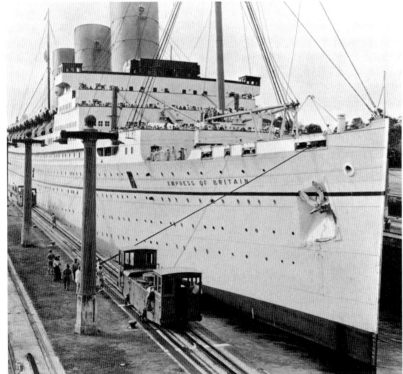

ABOVE
The thrill of a lifetime… through the Panama Canal en route to Europe on the *Empress of Britain*. The general belief is that in passing through the Panama Canal from the pacific to the Atlantic, ships travel from west to east. That is incorrect. The direction is north-west. The Pacific entrance to the Canal is 27 miles east of the exit on the Atlantic.

LEFT
The *Empress of Britain* was the largest ship of her time to use the Panama Canal.

OPPOSITE ABOVE
On the Panama Canal in 1931.

before the ship headed out into the Pacific, towards the Hawaiian Islands. Five idyllic days were spent at sea before arrival in Honolulu on 12 March, and on 15 March the Empress arrived in Hilo. On 20 March the *Empress of Britain* was the largest liner to sail through the Golden Gate and into San Francisco harbour. She berthed at the Embarcadero's Pier 32, and for the next two days was visited by several thousand people. This was followed by a call at Los Angeles, and then she went down the coast of Central America to the Panama Canal. Here, again, the *Empress of Britain* set a record, becoming at that time the largest liner to transit the canal, and thus incurring a fee of $18,941.25. Following the transit, 5 hours were spent at Cristobal before the ship set sail for Havana, the last exciting and exotic port of the

Passing Morro Castle on the entrance to Havana, Cuba.

cruise. The morning of 8 April was cold and grey, as the *Empress of Britain* made her way into her berth at one of New York's Manhattan piers. For the majority of her passengers this most remarkable cruise was at an end, but for the 100 European passengers there were still a few more days left, the crossing of the Atlantic to Southampton, and they were joined by a further 350 regular passengers for this final part of the voyage. The four-month

cruise was regarded as a success and most arrangements for the next World Cruise, scheduled to depart in just eight months time from New York on 3 December, were already in place.

Once back in Southampton the Empress was given a one-month overhaul and refurbishment in preparation for her forthcoming Atlantic season, and this of course included having her two propellers reattached. With the

OPPOSITE
She returned to Southampton for a refit and to have her second pair of propellers refitted for the beginning of her Atlantic season. Here she is photographed from the river Itchen at Woolston.

RIGHT
Two views of the *Empress of Britain* being repainted and touched up, taken at Southampton's western docks on 22 July 1936.

BELOW
Another view of the *Empress of Britain* at Southampton, showing her cruiser stern and aft docking bridge.

The substitution of oil fuel for coal has revolutionised modern marine machinery.

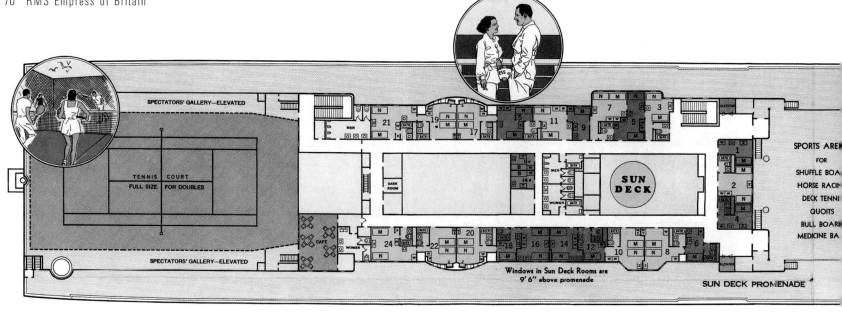

SPECTATORS' GALLERY—ELEVATED

TENNIS COURT
FULL SIZE FOR DOUBLES

SPECTATORS' GALLERY—ELEVATED

DARK ROOM

SUN DECK

CAFE

Windows in Sun Deck Rooms are
9' 6" above promenade

SPORTS AREA
FOR
SHUFFLE BOA
HORSE RACIN
DECK TENNI
QUOITS
BULL BOARI
MEDICINE BA

SUN DECK PROMENADE

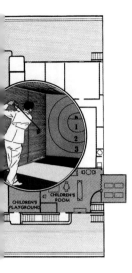

CLOCKWISE FROM TOP LEFT

The Sports Deck.

Tennis enthusiasts kept trim while cruising.

The Tennis Court Café.

To play long delightful games of tennis
in mid-ocean!

RIGHT
'*Empress of Britain* to Europe' – a clever way to
sell the last segment of the World Cruise.

effects of the Depression still being felt and consequently affecting the numbers of people travelling, Canadian Pacific reduced the minimum one-way first-class fare to $200. Perhaps the most significant event of the 1932 transatlantic season for the *Empress of Britain* was her fourth westbound crossing. On board were delegates from Britain, India, South Africa and Southern Rhodesia, who were to attend the Ottawa Imperial Economic Conference that would open on 21 July. Among them were Neville Chamberlain and Stanley Baldwin. As a result of the daily meetings of the 'miniature cabinet of seven', a stream of publicity was created, making the voyage world news. The voyage became even more news worthy on the evening of 17 July when, with the ship steaming slowly through fog and ice-bergs, a fire broke out in the ceiling of the Empress Room during a concert. The concert was brought to an abrupt end and the passengers filed from the room without any panic, and stewards and a watchman extinguished the fire, which was later discovered to have been caused by an electrical fault. The damage was confined to some woodwork and curtains. Fog, which had been a continual problem during the voyage, descended again as the ship was steaming up the St Lawrence, and on the morning of 18 July, as the ship was just off the Saguenay River, she collided with the cargo ship, *Briarwood*. A head-on collision was narrowly averted and the collision was described as having been 'a glancing blow.' Nevertheless, it left both ships with dents in their starboard bows but, as neither were in any danger, both continued with their respective voyages. The *Empress of Britain* was repaired by 20 July,

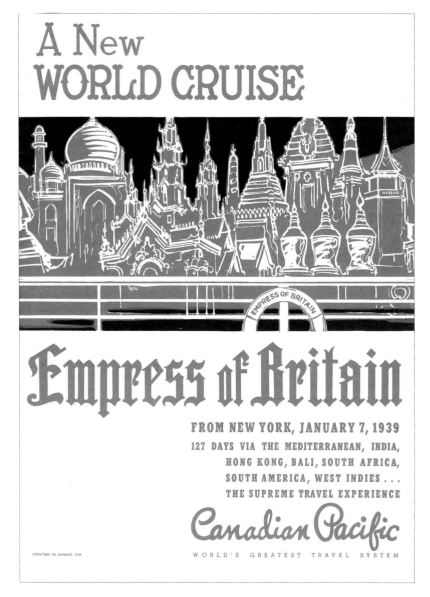

Her last ever World Cruise – 127 days from New York.

before she began her return voyage. The remaining Atlantic voyages of that year were fortunately less eventful and, at the end of that Atlantic season, she had carried a little over 11,000 passengers. So, despite her enviable reputation for luxury, speed and reliability, the *Empress of Britain* was still failing to fulfil her full potential – a fact that was undeniably a direct result of the world situation at the time.

On 23 November the *Empress of Britain* departed Southampton for New York with just 276 passengers aboard, ready to undertake her second cruise around the world. It was, in fact, the tenth World Cruise to be operated by the company and it was set to follow the same route as the previous cruise, only on this occasion it was of 129 days' duration and called at eighty-one ports and places in twenty-three countries and, as before, Canadian Pacific were promoting Christmas in the Holy Land, New Year's Eve in Cairo and India in the cool season. The most luxurious accommodations aboard, suites 144-146-148 and 147-149-151, were priced at $25,000 per suite for two people. Two modest inside cabins, forward on D Deck, were priced at the minimum fare of $2,300 per person: still an unattainable fortune to those in the ever-increasing dole queues. The Empress departed New York at noon on Saturday 3 December with barely 300 passengers aboard, a hundred of whom were only travelling as far as either the Mediterranean or India. Sixty passengers, including the playwright George Bernard Shaw, joined the ship at Monte Carlo. It was not until 11 April 1933 that the Empress steamed back into New York harbour and, by the middle of the month she was back again in Southampton, being made ready for another transatlantic season.

The effects of the Depression were such that Canadian Pacific had felt it necessary to withdrawn three of their liners, *Montcalm*, *Montclare* and *Montrose*, from the Liverpool–Canada service and place them on full-time cruise service. Of course Canadian Pacific was not the only steamship company to be suffering. Other companies were withdrawing ships, some of the most famous liners being rather downgraded to operating cheap short cruises; any employment being better than having the ships swing idly at anchor in some backwater. Work on the huge new Cunard liner at the John Brown yard remained at a standstill while the construction of the new liner for the French Compagnie Generale Transatlantique, which had been cut back to allow for a later delivery date of the ship, had only just resumed its original pace. It was a bleak time for everyone and all the shipping lines. Those shipping companies particularly hard hit were those aimed at the middle and lower end of the market, to the passengers already on a tight budget. Those were the potential passengers who, more than others, had to

CLOCKWISE FROM LEFT

'Hours and hours of happiness.'

On a cruise there was never a dull moment onboard.

A popular meeting place was the spacious Lounge Deck Square.

carefully watch their money, whereas those passengers who naturally travelled first class still frequented the opulent liners, albeit in lesser numbers than in previous years. Thus, the primarily first-class *Empress of Britain* departed Southampton on 3 May on her first Atlantic crossing to Canada of 1933 with only 345 passengers aboard. There were a mere 253 first-class passengers aboard during an August sailing, this at the very height of the season, and as the season came towards its close there were sometimes fewer than 300 in all three classes combined aboard. The *Empress of Britain* arrived in Southampton on 14 November, her season of Atlantic sailings at an end, and she had carried just 157 passengers more than in the previous year. However, the *Empress of Britain* was not alone crossing to and fro less than half full, and she was but only one of around seventy-five liners then employed on the North Atlantic.

For the end of 1933 Canadian Pacific had planned a change to the cruise programme of the *Empress of Britain*. Instead of sending her off in early December on her World Cruise, it was decided to begin that cruise in early January, and send the ship on an eleven-day Christmas and New Year cruise,

from New York to Kingston, Port-au-Prince and Nassau instead. The Empress had arrived in New York on 21 December with 319 passengers aboard, which in actual fact, in mid-December on a liner not regularly scheduled to sail on the New York run, in the depths of the Depression, was not a bad figure at all, especially when one considers that she had carried no more than that number on her regular employment on the St Lawrence service in the very height of the season. Planning to send the Empress on the Christmas cruise was a wise move as it was well patronised with passengers from both the United States and Canada. Apart from the crossings from Panama to Cuba during her two World Cruises, this was the *Empress of Britain*'s first real visit into the Caribbean. As always, wherever this most remarkable of liners called, she was an object of considerable interest.

The Empress returned to New York on the 2 January 1934, and embarkation for the 130-day World Cruise began the following morning,

with almost 300 passengers coming aboard. For them, once they stepped aboard, any ugly image of the Depression such as might have impinged upon their privileged lives, ceased to exist. Pampered by the ever-attentive Canadian Pacific crew (whose number far exceeded that of the number of passengers carried) for four months they would live a dream-like existence aboard this liner that by this time had begun to acquire an almost legendary status, and would be feted like royalty wherever they called. As was now becoming a regular pattern, around 100 passengers joined the ship at Monte Carlo. While the itinerary of the cruise was very similar to the previous two, the beautiful island of Bali had been included in the 1934 route. On 14 May she was back in New York, another World Cruise completed.

The most notable event for the *Empress of Britain* during 1934 was the retirement of Captain Latta. He had been her Master since the liner entered

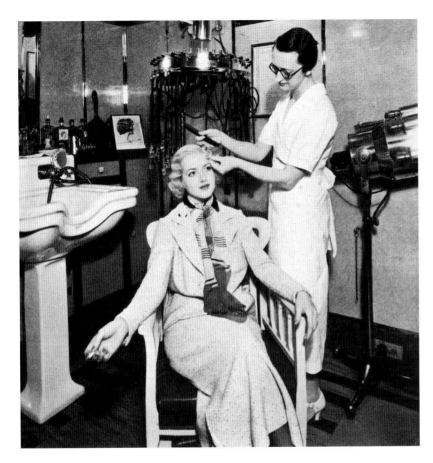

pay out any dividends to its shareholders. Nevertheless, the most expensive suites and most luxurious cabins for the *Empress of Britain*'s 1935 World Cruise were selling faster than the less expensive accommodation, giving perhaps a hint that maybe the worst of the Depression was coming to an end and that once again people were beginning to feel more relaxed about travelling.

However, it was a mere 180 passengers that boarded the liner for her voyage across the Atlantic to New York. On this voyage, as well as a considerable quantity of mail, she was transporting $1 million in gold. It was a stormy crossing, delaying her arrival by a day.

Such was the success of the cruise to the West Indies the previous year that Canadian Pacific scheduled the liner to undertake two similar cruises before sailing off on her World Cruise. The first of these was a four-day trip to Nassau, and this was followed by an eleven-day cruise to Kingston, Havana and Nassau. On 10 January 1935, with over 400 passengers aboard, the *Empress of Britain* sailed from New York for the Mediterranean on the first leg of her 130-day cruise around the world. As with the previous cruises, there were lengthy stays of several days in some of the ports. By 28 May she was, however, back in Southampton, another successful voyage around the world completed, and another season on the St Lawrence service to be made ready for.

On her first voyage to Canada in 1935 the *Empress of Britain* had just 318 passengers aboard, 125 of them in first class; there were also 7,000 bags of mail in her holds. A thick blanket of fog hung over the Gulf of St Lawrence, reducing shipping to a virtual standstill. However, the Empress managed to reach Quebec by 7.45 a.m. on 15 June, two days behind schedule. The passengers were disembarked and the dockworkers managed to unload all her cargo, and a further 550 passengers boarded in remarkably quick time, allowing the liner to sail again for England at 2.30 p.m. Unfortunately, the fog in the gulf had persisted and the following morning, when between Anticosti Island and the Magdalen Islands, the *Empress of Britain* collided with the cargo ship *Kafiristan*, which was loaded with coal. While the Empress sustained some hull damage, it was not serious. *Kafiristan*, however, was not so lucky and several crew members, who were asleep in their accommodation in her forecastle, were badly injured. The *Empress of Britain* stood by the damaged ship for several hours and, during this time, sent a boat across to collect the injured seamen. Sadly, as they were being helped into the boat, three of the men fell into the sea and were drowned. Another Canadian Pacific ship, the *Beaverford*, took the cargo ship in tow, and the *Empress of Britain* was then able to continue on her voyage. Although the

service, and his final voyage in command of the Empress was her 30 June departure from Quebec. His successor was Captain Ronald N. Stuart, VC, DSO. In August the Empress again made a record-breaking crossing, with a voyage between Quebec and Cherbourg made in just 4 days, 6 hours and 58 minutes. A month later the Empress encountered the worst weather and roughest seas of her career. While the North Atlantic is not unknown for its sometimes tempestuous conditions, the weather encountered as the liner made her way from Southampton to Quebec that September was quite remarkable: it was bitterly cold, and there was a combination of fog, snow and rain, and high winds causing heavy seas. The conditions conspired to ensure that this was not one of her speedy crossings. In November she briefly ran aground while at Quebec but was refloated within half-an-hour. It had, however, been an unsuccessful year, financially, for the company that advertised itself as 'The World's Greatest Travel System' and it had been unable to collision was seen as unavoidable, the *Empress of Britain* would eventually be held largely to blame. On her arrival in Southampton workmen from Harland & Wolff's repair yard spent 22 hours carrying out repairs, and she was able to return to service barely a day behind schedule.

While the *Empress of Britain* had carried in excess of 700 passengers on some of her crossings by the late summer of 1935, her passenger compliment was sometimes less than 300 and, on one occasion, it was as few as 184. However, overall she had carried 10,604 passengers on her Atlantic service, which was marginally more than in the previous year. While still sailing at less than half capacity it turned out to be the best financial year for the liner since having entered service. It was during that summer that reports began to circulate, perhaps inspired by the increase in passenger numbers, that Canadian Pacific were planning to build a sister ship. The company could see that this was just not realistic and openly stated that to build such a ship was not economically feasible.

Canadian Pacific had fully expected that the *Empress of Britain* would again follow her usual route around the world during those first four months of 1936. However, it was not to be, for in October 1935 Italy had invaded Abyssinia, and this caused several steamship companies to reconsider sending their ships through the Mediterranean and the Red Sea during their World Cruises. The alternative was to re-route their ships via South Africa, and this was what Canadian Pacific decided to do. However, not wanting to have two large liners cruising in the same part of the world at the same time, they cancelled the *Empress of Australia*'s planned South Africa and South America cruise, sending her on a series of shorter cruises to the West Indies instead.

As was now becoming a regular pattern of employment, the *Empress of Britain* sailed first on a nine-day Caribbean cruise, and embarked 610 passengers for this. The hostilities in the eastern Mediterranean/Red Sea and the consequent change to the World Cruise itinerary may well have affected bookings because the *Empress of Britain* sailed from New York with just 240 passengers. A further 100 British and continental passengers joined the ship at Funchal, having sailed there aboard the *Empress of Australia*, which was on her way to New York. The *Empress of Britain* caused quite a stir when she arrived in Cape Town, with huge crowds lining the docks to greet her. A strong south-east wind later

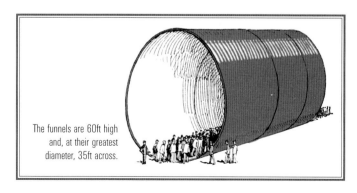

The funnels are 60ft high and, at their greatest diameter, 35ft across.

hindered her departure, holding her firmly against the dock. Several tugs were eventually able to get the liner underway, 24 hours behind schedule. Having made calls at Cape Town and Durban, the *Empress of Britain* steamed up to Bombay, and from there resumed her more usual route around the world.

In 1936 the number of passengers carried by the *Empress of Britain* rose considerably and on three westbound voyages she carried over 1,000 and with some eastbound sailings she also reached close to that number. There was also an increase in the number of passengers booking on the World Cruise, and on 9 January 1937 she sailed from New York with over 400 passengers aboard. The *Empress of Britain* was, by this time, truly well established as the pre-eminent World Cruise liner: the largest, newest, most opulent and indeed, the most expensive. As a consequence, on these fabled cruises her passenger lists read like a combination of *Debretts*, the *Almanac de Gotha* and *Who's Who*, with royalty, other titled aristocrats and business moguls as well as the merely very rich. Many of these people returned to the Empress year after year, giving the ship a very exclusive and club-like atmosphere. She was now under the command of Captain G.R. Parry and he remained as her master until October 1937, when Captain W.G. Busk-Wood took over.

At last there seemed to be a real change, with 1937 having been the best Atlantic season for the *Empress of Britain* as she carried in excess of 13,000 passengers between June and November. Although the *Empress of Britain* operated very speedy crossings, Canadian Pacific were operating at something of a handicap. Although the *Empress of Australia* was also employed on the Southampton–Quebec service as well, being an older and far slower ship, they were unable to offer a balanced service.

Canadian Pacific had expected that the 1938 World Cruise would resume its more usual route and produced publicity material to this effect. However, due to the continued conflict between China and Japan, once again they were forced to rethink the itinerary and decided to send the Empress to Australia and New Zealand instead. Prior to her departure on the World Cruise she had made a twelve-day cruise to the Caribbean. As usual, during the World Cruise, the *Empress of Britain* caused a stir wherever she called and it was estimated that over 30,000 people lined Sydney's waterfront when she arrived for her three-day stay. She was the largest liner to enter the harbour and, as her masts were too tall to allow her to pass under the harbour bridge, she docked at Wooloomooloo. After a call at Melbourne she steamed across the Tasman Sea to New Zealand, calling first at Wellington and then on to Auckland, where the harbour had had to be specially dredged to accommodate her 32ft draft.

The year 1938 did not continue to maintain the successes that had been achieved in 1937 for Canadian Pacific. Political unrest in Europe affected the numbers of people travelling from Canada and the United States that summer, and neither Australia nor New Zealand had held the same allure as China and Japan for would-be World Cruise passengers. Indeed, the company were faced with a real dilemma as the war between China and Japan continued, and they needed to plan the 1939 World Cruise. Then, in the spring of 1938, it had seemed that the hostilities might just be at an end, and the company bravely announced that the *Empress of Britain* would call at both countries the following year. Within just three months the hostilities had resumed and a new itinerary had to be planned. Although still calling at many of her regular ports, the company devised a very interesting and imaginative 127-day itinerary which, although promoted in a lavishly illustrated 70pp brochure as being a World Cruise, would mean that the Empress would not, on this occasion, encircle the globe.

It was planned that she would depart New York on 7 January, crossing the Atlantic to Madeira, Gibraltar, Algiers and Monte Carlo. There would then be the ever-popular calls at Naples and Athens, and the usual extended stay that allowed passengers to tour the Holy Land. Then onward to Suez, the Red Sea towards India, with a call of several days at Bombay. From there her passengers could take tours to Udaipur, Jaipur, Amber, Delhi, Agra, Benares, Darjeeling, Calcutta and Madras, and even cross over to Ceylon and re-board the Empress at Colombo. From there she would cross the Indian Ocean to Penang, Singapore and Bangkok, and on up to Hong Kong. Having called at Manila, Bali and Tandjong Priok on Java, the Empress was then to return across the Indian Ocean to South Africa, calling at Durban and Cape Town. From both those ports there were extensive overland tours up as far as Bulawayo and the Victoria Falls. After leaving Cape Town the

Tied up at the Western Docks, Southampton.

Empress of Britain was to head across the South Atlantic to St Helena, and then continue on to Rio de Janeiro. It would be the first time that she had called at a South American port. The brochure stated: 'And now for one of those swoops across the blue that makes us glad we're on the *Empress of Britain*, where no day is ever dull, no evening lacking in pleasant surprises. We rest, read, play, to tune our minds and bodies up for one of life's major thrills – RIO!' A call was made at Bahia and then up to Trinidad and finally Havana. Again, to quote the brochure: 'And now for Rhumba-Town, last and gayest port of call on all the cruise.' One entire page of the brochure was headed 'Suggested Preparatory Reading' and stated: 'Most travellers desire to acquaint themselves with the customs and history of the foreign lands they are to visit. The following comprehensive list of books is given in order that those who care to do so may prepare themselves by a course of reading prior to sailing.' Listed were 155 books. Having announced the cruise itinerary and issued the brochure, Canadian Pacific were then faced with what they referred to as 'upset political conditions' in the Holy Land. As a consequence the call there had to be cancelled, with the Empress being re-routed to Beirut instead. Despite the imaginative and exciting itinerary, passengers appeared to be reluctant to book the cruise.

The *Empress of Britain* was now under the command of Captain Charles Howard Sapsworth, the man who would have the sad honour of being her final master. Strong westerly gales delayed the arrival of the *Empress of Britain* in New York by 24 hours. On 23 December she sailed on a four-day Christmas cruise to Bermuda. On board were 650 passengers, all set to have a truly festive time. Following this, a further 600 passengers boarded the liner for an eight-day cruise to Havana, Nassau and Bermuda. However, it was a mere handful of passengers that had been enticed by the alternative World Cruise. Just 164 boarded the Empress on 7 January and, while more were due to board at Monte Carlo she would still be sailing with far fewer than the 400 that Canadian Pacific saw as the ideal World Cruise complement. However, a further 100 did join the ship at Cape Town, taking advantage of a far more luxurious way of getting to New York than the ships regularly employed on the route.

Canadian Pacific had planned for the *Empress of Britain* to undertake twenty-two Atlantic crossings during 1939. However, things did not work out quite as they had initially planned. On 6 May, King George VI and the Queen had embarked upon the *Empress of Australia* for a voyage to Canada for a royal tour of the Dominion. At the conclusion of the tour the royal party were to return aboard the *Empress of Britain*, and considerable preparations were made to ensure that everything was even beyond Canadian Pacific's normal flawless standards. The *Empress of Britain* had made her first crossing of the season to Quebec and, having disembarked her passengers, sailed for Halifax to be made ready for her special guests. The King was to occupy the de luxe suite on the port side of A Deck, while the Queen was in the corresponding suite on the starboard side. With the royal party aboard, the *Empress of Britain* left Halifax at 6.32 p.m. on 15 June: she had just forty-two passengers aboard; the King and Queen, thirty-seven staff members, a photographer and two reporters. Three ships of the Royal Navy and two of the Royal Canadian Navy accompanied the liner across the Atlantic. On 21 June, around 100 miles from Bishops Rock, the *Empress of Britain* passed the outbound *Empress of Australia*, and a message was sent from His Majesty the King to her passengers, officers and crew: 'We are delighted to see the *Empress of Australia* so close. We have many happy memories of our trip to Canada on her. Best of luck to you all.' A reply was received: 'We humbly beg to present our thanks for your generous message.' The following day the *Empress of Britain*, with her illustrious passengers, arrived in Southampton.

The royal charter of the liner had somewhat disrupted her schedule and it was not until 1 July that she was able to resume regular sailings, embarking 435 passengers for that particular voyage. Although plans had been drawn up for the Empress to undertake another World Cruise during the first four months of 1940, in August Canadian Pacific announced that this would not go ahead and, instead, after making three cruises to the Caribbean, the *Empress of Britain* would sail on a six-week cruise around South America. As the summer progressed the situation in Europe worsened. The *Empress of Britain* was being made ready to sail on 2 September on another voyage to Quebec but for a while it seemed that the Admiralty might not allow her to sail. Permission was, however, granted and with her portholes covered and public room windows blacked out, she sailed with 1,140 passengers. The following day they heard over the ship's radio the news that everyone had been expecting: Britain had declared war on Germany.

The *Empress of Britain* arrived in Quebec on 7 September and, having disembarked her passengers, remained there to await further instructions.

Their Majesties King George VI and Queen Elizabeth are seen here as they say farewell to Canada from the bridge of the Empress at Halifax, Nova Scotia, on 20 June 1939…

…and the ship is seen here from an escorting cruiser.

TRAGEDY

General location fair-sized trading vessel, approximately 20,000 tons, attacked successfully, there will be losses, listing, the boats are down.

Initial report made by the radio operator aboard the Focke-Wulf Condor 200 after the attack on the *Empress of Britain*.

The *Empress of Britain* remained in Quebec until November when she sailed for Halifax, Nova Scotia, never to be seen in the St Lawrence again. She had been requisitioned by the Ministry of War Transport, for like many large and fast ocean liners her potential as an effective troop transport was quickly realised. The Empress embarked troops from the First Canadian Division for an Atlantic voyage quite unlike any other of her career. Although having been given an all-over coat of grey paint and fitted with some limited amount of armament – a 6in naval gun and a 3in anti-aircraft gun at her stern four Lewis machine guns on her bridge and one either side of her second funnel – internally the Empress still gleamed in her pre-war opulence. The troops that she embarked went to war in luxury, enjoying the full benefit of Canadian Pacific's high standard of service. On 10 December, in company with the liners *Empress of Australia*, *Duchess of Bedford*, *Aquitania* and *Monarch of Bermuda*, the *Empress of Britain* departed on her first convoy; the liners, with their valuable cargo of troops, were escorted across the Atlantic to Scotland by Canadian and British destroyers.

Once the troops had been disembarked the *Empress of Britain* was sent to Southampton where she was dry docked and changed internally so that she could accommodate more troops, her larger cabins being fitted to take as many as twelve men. Her days as a luxury liner were truly over. Sadly, her fine panelling and artwork were only ever covered over with protective panels rather than being totally removed. With the hasty refitting work completed she returned to Halifax to embark more troops, also taking them across to Scotland. At the completion of that voyage she again sailed for Southampton and then left for New Zealand via the Mediterranean, arriving in Wellington on 14 April 1940. There she embarked troops of the 2nd New Zealand Expeditionary Force. The *Aquitania*, *Empress of Japan* and *Andes* were also there embarking troops, and the four liners, plus some cargo vessels, all departed in convoy on 2 May. When off Sydney, the convoy was joined by the liners *Queen Mary*, *Mauretania* and the *Empress of Canada*, making it one of the most impressive of the war. Having sailed from Fremantle it took the convoy two weeks to reach Cape Town.

The *Empress of Britain* was back on the Clyde by mid-June and remained there for some weeks, her next voyage beginning from Liverpool on 6 August, with over 3,000 troops aboard. Again, she was sailing in convoy with another array of once-splendid liners, including the *Monarch of Bermuda*

<hr />

At Quebec, where she was painted in her wartime Admiralty grey to begin her life as a troopship.

Empress of Britain, shown here in happier times, was sent to Southampton to be refitted for the carrying of huge quantities of troops.

and the Polish liner, *Batory*. Although the convoy was bound for Suez, they faced a long voyage around South Africa to get there. Once Italy had entered the war it had become far too dangerous for convoys of liners loaded with soldiers to sail through the Mediterranean. On 16 September the convoy arrived at Suez, and the Empress remained there until the twenty-fourth, when she became part of another convoy heading for Durban. This time, however, instead of thousands of troops, she was carrying a small passenger load, many of who were families of Army and Royal Air Force personnel. After her call at Durban the *Empress of Britain* sailed for Cape Town and there she took on a cargo of 300 tons of sugar. It has also been often reported that she had taken on a quantity of gold bullion. This fact, however, has never been substantiated. She sailed on 11 October for Britain with 224 military personnel and civilians and a crew of 419 aboard. The voyage was uneventful, the Empress maintaining a zigzagging course at 22 knots, without an escort due to her high speed.

Saturday 26 October was a fine day, there were a few clouds, a modest breeze, and the sea had a slight swell. The Empress was almost home, just sixty miles off the north-west coast of Ireland; she was expected to reach port within the day.

At 9.20 a.m. the lookout spotted a four-engined plane approaching, and then circle the liner: it was at first thought to be 'friendly.' It was in fact a German long-range Focke-Wulf Condor 200. Having circled the speeding Empress it made its first approach from her stern, dropping two bombs and raining machine gun fire onto her. Captain Sapsworth had called for full speed and the Empress was steaming at 24 knots, returning fire from her Lewis guns, which managed to inflict some damage to the plane: rupturing an oil line and putting an engine out of action. Despite this, the Focke-Wulf remained a lethal adversary, returning for another attack, but already the Empress was filling with thick black smoke, one of the bombs having penetrated the former Mayfair Lounge. The Empress was burning. Two more bombs were dropped from the plane, neither finding their mark. The next time the pilot turned his plane to approach the Empress from her bow, raking the ship with machine-gun fire and dropping yet two more bombs, one of which struck the Sun Deck, destroying several lifeboats and creating more fires. The other bomb hit the a ship near to her stern, which put the anti-aircraft gun out of action, creating a fire that caused the stored ammunition to explode. Yet again the pilot turned his plane to create more havoc upon the already crippled liner, this time spraying machine-gun fire across her bridge. The Focke-Wulf then turned away to the south, her pilot sending out signals indicating the position of the burning liner.

It was only after Oberleutnant Jope had landed his plane at the base in northern France that he and his crew learned the true facts about the ship they had attacked and, as a result, there was a great deal of excitement. A telex, reporting the attack, was sent from Jope's unit to German Supreme Headquarters. Realising just how significant such an attack was, a reconnaissance plane was sent immediately to verify the report. Despite having done so, the official German news agency still reported that the *Empress of Britain* was already sunk, stating: 'The *Empress of Britain* was successfully attacked by German bombers on Saturday morning within the waters of Northern Ireland. The ship was badly hit and began to sink at once. The crew took to their boats.'

It was fortunate that, despite the ferocity of the attack and the subsequent fires, there were relatively few casualties. It was apparent to Captain Sapsworth that the once glorious Empress was now doomed: the fires had spread through several decks and, as the fire-fighting equipment had been damaged in the attack, they were beyond being brought under control. Thus, he gave the order to have the engines stopped and for the ship to be abandoned. From the sighting of the plane to the 'Abandon Ship' order a mere 30 minutes had elapsed: just half-an-hour to destroy Britain's most splendid liner. Once the crew felt assured that the plane would not return, those lifeboats that remained undamaged were made ready to be lowered to take the passengers and crew. While it had taken but 30 minutes to render the liner to a blazing hulk, it was nearly 6 hours before the last survivor was taken off the wrecked *Empress of Britain*.

Upon spotting the lone German bomber, Captain Sapsworth ordered full speed and, as the Empress sailed at 24 knots, she was raked with bombs.

Late that afternoon the first rescue ships arrived on the scene, the Polish destroyer *Burza* and the Royal Navy destroyer *Echo*, and arriving soon after them were three trawlers, *Cape Argona*, *Paynter* and *Drangey*. As the destroyers approached, huge sheets of flames shot up through the already devastated liner. They lowered their boats to pick up the survivors and later took aboard those that had been picked up by the trawlers. Once they had everyone aboard they were instructed to sail for the Clyde. Two further destroyers, *Broke* and *Sardonyx*, arrived to take their place.

It was very fortunate that out of the 643 people aboard, only forty-five were unaccounted for, and just thirty-two of those were members of the crew. It was presumed that unaccounted souls had either been killed outright, injured and then trapped by the fires, or that they had drowned.

Remarkably, considering the intensity of the attack and the subsequent explosions and fires aboard her, the hull of what remained of the *Empress of Britain* was still intact. Although she had a slight list, she appeared to be in no danger of sinking, therefore it was decided that it was worth trying to save her. On 27 October, the day after the attack, a party of men from the *Broke* went aboard and attached tow-ropes (dangerous work as the ship was still burning). The ocean-going tugs *Marauder* and *Thames* had arrived, and had the task of taking the gutted hulk of the once lovely Empress in tow. Slowly, under the care of the tugs, she began to move, *Broke* and *Sardonyx* standing by to act as escorts. The magnificent *Empress of Britain*, although ripped apart by explosions and gutted by fire, was not dead yet. Under the tender care of the salvage tugs and the watchful eyes of her escorting destroyers she could yet, with luck, make port. A ship of her capacity was a valuable asset during those dark days of war: she could be rebuilt, she needed to be rebuilt.

Good fortune had, however, deserted the Empress, for while she was under attack, the German submarine *U-32* was just 60 miles to the southwest. Her commander, Oberleutnant Hans Jenisch, had been informed, after the attack, of the location of the burning liner, and headed in that direction. Although he had spotted the limping Empress and her attendant tugs and destroyers, he had been unable to do anything other than order the U-boat to dive as there was a patrolling plane circling overhead. Later, when Jenisch ordered his craft to the surface, the Empress was nowhere to be seen but, that night, using passive sonar, he located the ships and closed in on them. The destroyers were maintaining a zigzagging course but *U-32* was able to get into position between them and the *Empress of Britain*, and fired two torpedoes. The first of these detonated prematurely but the second hit the devastated liner, causing a massive explosion. It appears that initially the crews of the destroyers assumed that the fires aboard the liner having reached her fuel tanks had caused the explosion. Although anxious to escape undetected, Jenisch ordered *U-32* around and fired another torpedo; it found its mark just aft of where the earlier one had exploded, ripping another hole in the hull of the Empress. Confident of his success, Jenisch ordered his submarine safely away from the scene.

The *Empress of Britain* was now mortally wounded, her hull rapidly filling through the gaping holes with seawater; she began to list heavily to port. The

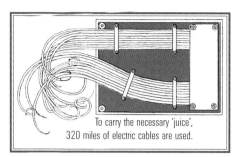

To carry the necessary 'juice', 320 miles of electric cables are used.

crews of the tugs rapidly let go the tow lines and, at 2.05 a.m. on Monday 28 October 1940, the *Empress of Britain* slipped beneath the waves of the North Atlantic, a mere half-a-day's sailing from the shipyard where she had been built. Britain's greatest liner was no more.

Her war service was not over though. As the largest wreck on the seabed off Britain and, in a known location, she was used to help rid the world of the U-boat menace. Boffins had been developing anti-submarine weapons, one of which was 'Hedgehog', a forward-thrown series of mortar bombs that proved to be a successful weapon in the Battle of the Atlantic. The projectiles, fired over the bow from a navy vessel, sank in the approximate pattern of a submarine's shape. Only exploding on contact, the Hedgehog was designed to replace the less accurate depth charge. The mortar shells were designed to puncture and explode the pressure hull of a submarine and the Empress was the target for the development of this weapon. Her wreck is most likely surrounded by unexploded ordnance and covered in nets from the trawlers that use this area for fishing.

IN THE WAKE OF AN EMPRESS

Those of us who knew that magnificent British ship will not forget her easily. She was unique of her class, great in size yet not a monster, modern in line but in no way freakish, powerful and sturdy but of a graceful symmetry, solid and steady in action yet flexible in movement to the waves that bore her. She was a real ship of the sea, fashioned by a race of shipbuilders, her name, appearance and significance known and respected all over the world which she had circled so many times. She will not be forgotten. Indeed it is safe to guess that one day she will live again, for surely Canada will recreate for her a daughter, in her own name and something like her own image, a daughter perhaps even more beautiful than the mother.

Words spoken by the actor, Leslie Howard, during his talk in the BBC radio series *Britain Speaks*, on 4 November 1940.

On Monday 28 October 1940, newspapers reported a British Government communiqué as saying that the *Empress of Britain* had been bombed and had sunk following an explosion while the vessel was being towed to port. On 5 November a further report implied that the final blow had been struck by a submarine, which torpedoed the ship as she was being towed from the scene of the aerial attack.

In the words of one of the crew, as reported by the *Toronto Daily Star*: 'In no time at all the ship was a mass of thick choking smoke – we couldn't see.

We tried to beat out the flames, which were steadily gaining. We all stood by our posts until the order to leave the ship was sounded. I and two other fellows tried to get at the boat deck but the dense smoke drove us back. We were forced to put on our gas masks. Only for them we would never have been able to get to the boats and get them away. By this time many of them were afire. After the bomber had dropped his missiles he circled the ship and machine-gunned the passengers and crew. The chief officer was wounded in the leg by machine-gun bullets and also a piece of shrapnel in the back, yet he carried on in the work of rescue. Twenty-two officers and men tried to get away in a motor launch, which had been afire. We came alongside and took off an injured man. A short time later the launch capsized when it filled with water – it had been peppered with machine-gun bullets. Eight of them were saved. After leaving the ship we went around and picked up survivors who had jumped overboard or who were hanging on ladders. I fell into a lifeboat when the ladder I was climbing down burned away. We drifted around from 11.00 a.m. until 5.00 p.m., when two destroyers came to our rescue. Some of those who jumped over the side died of exposure right away. Those in the boats kept their spirits high singing. It was my first ship, and to see her go down was like losing your best friend.'

Sir Edward Beatty, GBE, KC LL.D, chairman and president of Canadian Pacific Railway, issued the following statement: 'News of the loss of the *Empress of Britain* will come to the great army of people who have travelled aboard her very much as would that of the loss of a personal friend, while all

Canadians will hear with a feeling of deep regret that the gallant ship which for nine years proudly represented Canada in all the world's great ports has met her fate at the hands of the enemy. The *Empress of Britain* was designed and built to help maintain for the St Lawrence gateway to Canada a position of high importance among the world's ocean ports, and splendidly she accomplished that duty. She had many proud moments in her all too short career. Those who saw her first entry into Quebec harbour will not forget the tremendous demonstration that greeted her. That was an event second only in interest to the day the ship bore Their Majesties the King and Queen from Halifax on their way home. To the Canadian Pacific Steamship Co. her loss brings an especially keen regret. We were proud of her beauty and of her consistently fine performance and we had reason also to be gratified by the fact that, while her building might have been termed a bold experiment, it was seen to be thoroughly justified very early in her career. The ship has met her end gallantly in the service of the country, as have many others, but when the war is finished and won, still others equally as fine will be built to take their places and carry on the work of maintaining our British supremacy on the seas. Of the loss of the forty-five passengers and crew one can only speak with sorrow, which may be somewhat mitigated by pride in the fact that they went to their death with their faces bravely turned towards their duty, as is the manner of British seamen. To their relatives and friends will go the country's heartfelt sympathy.'

During the following days other equally fulsome tributes were paid to the *Empress of Britain*. The Prime Minister of Canada, the Rt Hon.

W.L. Mackenzie King said: 'She will long be remembered by Canadians as a brave ship who did her duty in peace and war. Canadians have heard with profound regret of the loss of the *Empress of Britain*, and with pride of the heroic conduct of her officers and men. For many years she carried the name and fame of Canada with high honour into most of the world's great ports. When war broke out she was assigned to the sterner tasks of war, and in those tasks played a memorable part. To the relatives of the heroic seamen who lost their lives when their ship sank in the Atlantic, I send the deepest sympathy of the people of Canada.'

The *KingstonWhig-Standard* of Kingston, Ontario, made the most poignant of statements: 'The sinking of the *Empress of Britain* removes the pride of Canada's merchant marine…' *Fairplay*, the London weekly shipping journal stated the very harsh fact: 'The *Empress of Britain* was one of the liners of the British mercantile marine we could ill afford to lose.' The report continued: 'She was considered by many good judges to be one of the most satisfactory ships ever turned out from Messrs John Brown's yard at Clydebank, which is, perhaps, as high praise as can be given to any vessel… That such a fine vessel should come to an end by being bombed, and that all the foresight of the company who ordered the ship, the skill of her designers, the honest craft of the workmen who fashioned her, and the ability and experience of the crew who ran her, should be wasted by this destruction, is perhaps, a negligible matter when viewed in the light of the other devastation which has been caused by Hitler and his satellites, but the effect is cumulative, and we may hope that the reckoning will take account of every item.'

In Montreal, *The Gazette* reported: 'Canadians will regret very deeply the destruction of the magnificent *Empress of Britain*, because she was the pride of the Canadian service, because she was symbolic of the growing greatness of the Dominion and reflected that greatness where ever she went.' Another Montreal newspaper, The *Montreal Daily Star*, stated: 'She was in very truth Canada's ambassador-at-large, known and admired throughout the Seven Seas. The gallantry of her captain and his officers and men was as we should have expected – true to the highest traditions of the British mercantile marine. This is our abiding solace. British ships and British seamen never fail us.'

OPPOSITE
In happier times, leaving Southampton, her hull resplendent in white.

RIGHT
The *Empress of Britain* was a pretty ship from almost any angle. This starboard profile shows her magnificent buff funnels and her gleaming hull off to perfection.

One of the finest ships built on the Clyde and, like another of John Brown's ocean greyhounds (*Lusitania*), destined to be sunk by submarine.

It was *The Daily Colonist*, of Victoria BC, that pointed out the tragic fact that the *Empress of Britain* was: '… the largest individual loss of tonnage yet inflicted at sea in warfare.' It went on to remind its readers that the Empress was ranked among the ten greatest vessels in the world at that time. Meanwhile, the *Toronto Globe and Mail* joined in the praise for the crew of the *Empress of Britain*: 'The loss is tempered by the gallant behaviour of the crew, who maintained the highest traditions of the sea for bravery and coolness. Captain Sapsworth stuck to the bridge, a target of Nazi machine-guns, until it was crumbling in flames. The fight put up in defence is one of which Britishers can be proud.' Other newspapers across Canada reported in similar vein: The *Quebec Chronicle-Telegraph* stated: '… How much more fitting that she should find a water grave in the service of her country than that she should be broken up for scrap metal, the fate that would normally have overtaken her.' The Ottawa newspaper, *The Citizen*, reminded its readers that along with the loss of the *Empress of Britain*, Canada had also lost one of its most formidable warships, the HMCS *Margaree*, during that same week. *The Halifax Mail* was rather more passionate: 'The loss of the *Empress of Britain* is one of the bitterest tragedies of this war. The destruction of this beautiful ship – the White Empress – is another foul crime to be charged to the black account of barbarism.'

New York, a city associated with all the greatest of ocean liners, paid its own special tribute in *The New York Times* on 29 October: 'No ship ever fitted her name more truly than the *Empress of Britain*. She was indeed an empress, with pride and grace and dignity in every inch of her…' The article recalled the role of the Empress, during both peace and war, and ended by saying: 'The memory of this fine ship will survive until a new *Empress of Britain* inherits her name.' It was, however, *The Winnipeg Tribune* that perhaps best evoked the image of the now lost ship and looked forward to the future: 'The loss of the *Empress of Britain* touches Canadians deeply. She was the pride of the Canadian merchant marine and there was no finer sight in the world than the lordly ship on the broad St Lawrence, steaming out to the highways of the world. But she served in war as proudly as in her ten years of peace. There are tales of her service as a troopship, carrying men of the Empire from the ends of the earth, to be told when the foul

LEFT TO RIGHT

Empress of Britain had five captains in her short ten year life. Captain Latta was her first commander, while Captain R.N. Stuart VC, DSO, RNR, USNC, was her second, from 1934.

Captain G.R. Parry took command in 1936 and was succeeded in 1937 by Captain W.G. Busk-Wood.

Captain Busk-Wood had sailed for many years on wooden walls but commanded the company's *Empress of Australia* as well as *Montcalm*, *Montrose* and *Duchess of Bedford*, before taking command of the largest ship in the CPR fleet.

Captain Sapsworth was responsible for the ship from 1937 until her sinking and was ultimately responsible for ensuring the saving of most of the crew and passengers when she was sunk.

How it could have been: the *Empress of Canada* on convoy duty in mid-Atlantic in March 1942, barely a year before she too was lost to a submarine.

menace to humanity is overcome, and men in ships can plow the sea once more as harbingers of good will, joining continents in the pursuit of peace.'

A tribute was also sent from Buckingham Palace to Sir Edward Beatty and Canadian Pacific: 'I have been asked by the King and Queen to convey to you and the directors of the Canadian Pacific Railway their sincere sympathy in the loss of that fine ship, the *Empress of Britain*, in which Their Majesties had such a pleasant voyage from Canada last year.' Sir Edward responded: 'I shall be very glad if you will be good enough to express to Their Majesties our directors' and my own deep appreciation of their kind message of sympathy in the loss of the *Empress of Britain*. She was a beautiful ship, of which all Canadians were very proud. In my judgement, she was one of the finest examples of the skill of the Clyde shipbuilders and she ended her life gloriously in the service of the nation.'

Just two days after having dealt the final blow to the *Empress of Britain*, *U-32* herself was sunk by the British destroyer *Harvester*. She and another destroyer, *Highlander*, picked up several members of the submarine's crew. Some time later, in one of those strange twists of fate, those same crew members were being transported from Britain to a prisoner of war camp in Canada, aboard a Canadian Pacific liner, the *Duchess of York*. She was under the command of none other than Captain Sapsworth!

On the afternoon of Sunday 10 November, a memorial service for the ship and her men was held in Montreal's church of St Andrew and St Paul. The church was filled with Montreal's prominent citizens and hundreds of others who had known the ship as passengers or as officers of the company she represented. In the course of his address Revd Dr Geo. H. Donald said: 'To the many thousands of passengers who had travelled on the *Empress of Britain* across the Atlantic or on cruises round the world, her loss was felt as that of a personal friend rather than as an inanimate vessel, magnificent though that vessel was. There is something intimate and personal about all ships but she was one of the greatest that sailed the Atlantic and the further

Dressed overall in flags, the third Canadian Pacific ship to bear the name *Empress of Britain* makes a triumphant maiden arrival into Liverpool on 10 April 1956.

Photographed in April 1956 in the Mersey, the last *Empress of Britain* shows her John Brown-built design off to perfection as seagulls fly over her forward cargo hatches.

The third *Empress of Britain* being berthed by tugs.

Empress of Britain off Southampton, 1931. The sender of this postcard was lucky enough to tour the splendours of the *Empress of Britain* during Southampton's Merchant Navy Week in 1937.

seas. The whole world was proud of her and mourns today as for one who died before her time.'

Canadian Pacific suffered badly during those years of the war, the loss of their flagship being just the beginning. Just two weeks after Jope's air attack on the *Empress of Britain*, they came close to losing their other prestigious liner, *Empress of Japan*. Once again it was an attack by an aircraft off the northern coast of Ireland. The ship was damaged when a bomb exploded under her stern. However, under the care of a destroyer she was able to make port and was repaired. Sadly, neither the *Empress of Asia* nor the *Empress of Canada* would be so lucky. The *Empress of Asia* was sunk during an air attack off Singapore on 5 February 1942, with the loss of nineteen lives. Just over a year later, on 14 March 1943, while on a voyage from Durban to England, the *Empress of Canada* was sunk by torpedoes fired from an Italian submarine. The *Duchess of Atholl* also fell victim to a torpedo attack in the south Atlantic, on 10 October 1942, when 200 miles off Ascension Island. Her sister ship, the *Duchess of York*, was attacked by German long-range bombers on 11 July 1943 off the Portuguese coast, and sank the following day.

With the war coming to a close, the *Empress of Russia* was withdrawn from war work and sent to the Barrow-in-Furness yard of Vickers-Armstrong. She was to be refitted to transport the wives and families of Canadian servicemen

from Britain to Canada. The work continued through most of the summer of 1945. Then, in the early hours of 8 September, a fire broke out in her accommodation, gutting the ship and leaving her beyond economic repair.

After the war, the directors of Canadian Pacific had every intention of a resumption of ocean liner services on both the Pacific and the Atlantic, and there were plans for two large new ships, one for each route. Nevertheless, they recognised that the demand was greater on the North Atlantic and that was where they needed to focus their operations. It has been reported that, to show its gratitude for its outstanding wartime services, Canada offered to build a similar-sized liner as the *Empress of Britain* as a gift to Canadian Pacific. However, perhaps seeing before them a new world, and appreciating the fact that even in the old one such a liner had been an expensive luxury, the offer was declined. Instead, the two liners *Duchess of Bedford* and *Duchess of Richmond* were both refitted and transformed into the *Empress of France* and *Empress of Canada* respectively. The *Empress of Scotland*, which had, up until the entry of Japan into the war, been known as the *Empress of Japan* was now the flagship of the fleet. However, the trio of liners only had a short time together on the service to the St Lawrence as on 25 January 1953, the *Empress of Canada* was destroyed by fire while being refitted at Liverpool. The French Line vessel, *De Grasse*, was hastily acquired and renamed *Empress of Australia*, making her first voyage for Canadian Pacific on 28 April, just three months after the *Canada* had been destroyed.

The ageing former French liner was just a stop-gap. Canadian Pacific was already in the process of planning a new liner, and the order was placed with the Fairfield Shipbuilding & Engineering Co. on the Clyde. In April 1954 it was announced that she would be the new *Empress of Britain* and would introduce a 'new look' to the company's fleet. She was launched by Her Majesty the Queen on 22 June 1955, and entered service the following April. The 'new look' liner had a low and modern profile and was of 26,000grt – considerably smaller than her illustrious predecessor. She was handsome, but not imposing; her public rooms and cabins were attractive but not opulent. While she carried the name *Empress of Britain* and served on the St Lawrence service – and had been designed with cruising in mind – she was not a direct replacement for the earlier ship. It was a different age and passengers had different requirements. She was followed in April 1957 by a virtually identical sister ship named *Empress of England*. Then, in April 1961, they were joined by the 27,300grt *Empress of Canada*: the last passenger liner to be built for Canadian Pacific.

All three liners divided their time between summers on the service between Britain and the St. Lawrence, and wintertime cruising. However, the three ships were not destined to sail together for long and, in fact, the new *Empress of Britain* sailed for an even shorter time for Canadian Pacific than her predecessor. With fewer and fewer passengers crossing the Atlantic by sea, the company decided that they could not justify a three-ship fleet and the *Empress of Britain* was sold, in February 1964, to Greek Line and became their *Queen Anna Maria*. The *Empress of England* remained with Canadian Pacific until 1970, when she was sold to Shaw Savill Line, becoming their *Ocean Monarch*. Her career with them was all too brief, and by the summer of 1975 she was sold to Taiwanese ship breakers. The *Empress of Canada* soldiered on alone and tried to maintain the glory that had been Canadian Pacific but it was not economic to maintain just one liner and, in November 1971, she made the final transatlantic sailing for the company. The operation of Canadian Pacific ocean liners was at an end.

In 1972 the *Empress of Canada* was sold and became the *Mardi Gras*, the first cruise ship for the fledgling company, Carnival Cruise Lines. In December 1975, after almost eleven months of lay-up following the collapse of Greek Line, the former *Empress of Britain*, now renamed *Carnivale*, joined her. Between them, these former Atlantic liners helped reshape and revitalise the cruise industry, both remaining as units of the Carnival fleet for over twenty years. By 1993 Carnival were looking to dispose of these now vintage liners. The former *Empress of Canada* never really operated with any real degree of success after then, except for two brief seasons sailing as *Apollon* for Direct Cruises out of Liverpool during 1998/99.

The *Empress of Britain*, however, continued to be blessed by success. Briefly, she was operated by the Greek company, Epirotiki Lines, as the *Olympic*. Then, acquired by a new owner, she was placed under a five-year charter to the British tour company Thomson's and sailed very successfully for them as *The Topaz* until April 2003. Shortly after, forty-seven years after her maiden voyage, she found another charter, with a Japanese educational organisation, Peace Boat, which operated her on a series of cruises around the world.

It is perhaps a strange irony that the (1931) *Empress of Britain* made her reputation as the most luxurious and prestigious liner operating cruises around the world, allowing the very rich escape the rigours of the winter, whereas the (1956) *Empress of Britain* ended her long career operating similar lengthy cruises, but for students seeking to learn about the world.

It is a sad fact that the splendour and luxury of the *Empress of Britain* of 1931 is somewhat overlooked, the ship being labelled instead as one of the least profit-making liners of her time. She was, however, conceived as a serious contender to those liners that regarded Manhattan as their terminus, and suffered as a consequence. Despite Canadian Pacific's boast of '39% less ocean' the sometime more tempestuous longer ocean route to New York remained the prestige service. A lone ship is always a liability but, after a short while of operating the liner, the directors of Canadian Pacific were well aware that a sister to the *Empress of Britain* would be an even greater liability. In his statement shortly after her loss, the Canadian Pacific chairman and president, Sir Edward Beatty, had alluded to the less than dazzling profits earned by the Empress by saying: '… while her building might have been termed a bold experiment, it was seen to be thoroughly justified very early in her career.' She was built and entered service in the early days of the Depression, then, as those days began to fade, Europe fell into political unrest and, ultimately, war. Like all the great liners of the 1930s, the odds were stacked against her. Nevertheless, the *Empress of Britain* was a most remarkable liner. One of the reporters that covered her arrival in Cape Town in 1936 put it quite simply: 'The *Empress of Britain* was the most beautiful ship I ever saw.'

Just ten short, glorious years were to separate this view of the *Empress of Britain* on the Clyde on her sea trials and her tragic demise as the biggest merchant loss of the Second World War.

RMS EMPRESS OF BRITAIN

Length (overall)	760ft 6in
Breadth	97ft 6in
Gross Tonnage	42,348
Shaft Horsepower	62,500
Normal Speed	24 knots

CAPACITY FOR PASSENGERS

First	465
Tourist	260
Third	470
Total	1,195
Officers and Crew	714
Port of Registry	London

Fastest passage steaming time, 4 days, 6 hours,
58 minutes, between Father Point, Quebec,
and Cherbourg, France, August 1934.

BIBLIOGRAPHY

Gordon Turner, *Empress of Britain* (Stoddart Publications & Boston Mills Press)

Robert Turner, *The Pacific Empresses* (Sono Nis Press)

Derek M. Whale, *The Liners of Liverpool Part II* (Countryvise Publications)

Clarence Winchester, *Shipping Wonders of the World* (The Amalgamated Press Ltd)

Frank O. Braynard & William H. Miller, *Fifty Famous Liners* Vol 1. (Patrick Stevens Ltd)

John Malcolm Brinnin & Kenneth Gaulin, *Grand Luxe, The Transatlantic Style* (Bloomsbury Publishing)

Arnold Kludas, *Great Passengers Ships of the World* (Patrick Stevens Ltd)

Robert Seamer, *The Floating Inferno* (Patrick Stevens Ltd)

Ocean Liners of the Past, Empress of Britain: reprint of *The Shipbuilder and Marine Engine-Builder*.